Presented to

Kait

By

Jud & Ann Price - We love you!

On the Occasion of

High School Graduation

Date

May 13, 2006

GOD'S GRADUATE

KAREN MOORE

CONTINUING EDUCATION *for* EVERYDAY LIFE

BARBOUR
PUBLISHING

ISBN 1-59789-071-5

Cover image: Jupiter Images
Design: studiogearbox.com

Published by Barbour Publishing, Inc., P.O. Box 719, Uhrichsville, Ohio 44683, www.barbourbooks.com

Our mission is to publish and distribute inspirational products offering exceptional value and biblical encouragement to the masses.

 Member of the
Evangelical Christian
Publishers Association

Printed in China.
5 4 3 2 1

Contents

1. Attitude 6
2. Beginnings and Endings 10
3. Being Yourself 17
4. Change 24
5. Choices 28
6. Courage 33
7. Effort 36
8. Excuses 40
9. Exploring 42
10. Failure 44
11. Faith 51
12. Family 58
13. Forgiveness 62
14. Friendship 66
15. Giving 70
16. Goals 74
17. God 78
18. Grace 86
19. Growth 92
20. Heart 96
21. Hope 101
22. Integrity 104
23. Kindness 109
24. Learning 116
25. Life 118
26. Light 128
27. Love 133
28. Nature 143
29. Patience 145
30. Peace 150
31. Prayer 153
32. Proverbs 158
33. Service 163
34. Success 168
35. Trials 172
36. Trust 175
37. Wisdom 178
38. Work 181
39. Worry 183

ATTITUDE

WHAT'S IMPOSSIBLE?

The "impossible can always be broken down into possibilities." Is there anything in your life that feels "impossible" today? If there is, then the trick is to try taking another approach. What if you take that word and break it into "im" and "possible" and take a little leap and go to "I'm possible"? With you in the picture, taking the obstacles and moving them one by one into manageable pieces, things change. You're the catalyst, the possibility mover and shaker, the one who makes a difference.

Norman Vincent Peale was totally a possibility thinker. He said it's always good to "become a possibilitarian. No matter how dark things seem to be or actually are, raise your sights and see possibilities—always see them, for they're always there."

It's possible that this could be a great day made just for you!

❈❈❈❈❈❈❈❈❈❈❈❈❈❈❈❈❈❈❈❈❈❈❈❈❈❈❈❈❈❈❈❈❈❈❈❈❈

CONTINUING EDUCATION

[Jesus told them,] "I assure you, even if you had faith as small as a mustard seed you could say to this mountain, 'Move from here to there,' and it would move. Nothing would be impossible."

MATTHEW 17:20

WHEN SKIES ARE GRAY

Whether we're talking about sunshine and rain or snow and ice, our attitude is what really determines the weather. When the weather of your life turns gray, check to see if there's any sunshine left in your attitude.

A. A. Milne put these words into Eeyore's mouth:

> "It's snowing still," said Eeyore gloomily.
> "So it is."
> "And it's freezing."
> "Is it?"
> "Yes," said Eeyore.
> "However," he said, brightening up a little,
>   "we haven't had an earthquake lately."

And James Whitcomb Riley put it yet another way:

> It is no use to grumble and complain;
> It's just as cheap and easy to rejoice;
> When God sorts out the weather and sends rain—
> Why, rain's my choice.

What's your choice today? It's all a matter of attitude!

CONTINUING EDUCATION

When the clouds are heavy, the rains come down.
When a tree falls, whether south or north, there it lies.
If you wait for perfect conditions, you will never get anything done.

ECCLESIASTES 11:3–4

HERE I AM; THERE YOU GO!

You've been around long enough now to observe that there are people who always seem to command attention when they enter a room. Sometimes they do it so quickly that you don't even realize you've been dismissed as they take over. Frederick Collins said, "There are two types of people—those who come into a room and say, 'Well, here I am!' and those who come in and say, 'Ah, there you are.'"

On graduation day, it's all about you, and it's okay to say, "Well, here I am." But most of the time, it's better to adopt an attitude of humility. Jesus even told the teachers of His day that those who exalted themselves would be brought down and those who humbled themselves would be exalted. It seems the best way to be the greatest is to be the best servant.

As you walk through the world today, create a space for everyone you meet so they can shine with you.

CONTINUING EDUCATION

When you bow down before the Lord and admit your dependence on him, he will lift you up and give you honor.

JAMES 4:10

LIFELONG LEARNING

Learning from experience is a lifelong pursuit without a graduation. No doubt you'll earn a Ph.D. before you're done, and sometimes you'll choose the courses to take and sometimes you won't. What kind of student will you be?

Students who remain at the top of the class are usually those who take any experience offered them and find a positive outcome to guide them in a future course of similar events. Since you've been there before, you feel more prepared for making choices the next time around.

What do you do when life hands you an experience that doesn't seem to have had a textbook prerequisite? What if you weren't prepared for it in any way? How you respond to the events of your life is as important, if not more so, than the events themselves.

The wisest students always know where to turn when life blindsides them. They know that they can rely on the Source, the Master Teacher, the Creator to see them through. Don't forget to raise your hand; in fact, raise both of your hands and thank God for being with you every day.

CONTINUING EDUCATION

Give your burdens to the LORD, and he will take care of you.
He will not permit the godly to slip and fall.

PSALM 55:22

BEGINNINGS AND ENDINGS

Graduation: Endings and Beginnings

The experience of a graduation is a two-edged sword. On one hand, you're thrilled to be finished with the hard work, the study, the papers, and the homework. On the other hand, a tremendous change is taking place. Classroom buddies you've come to associate with learning a particular subject will move out of your life. Teachers whom you've finally grown to understand will get new students. Moments you've shared with friends and times you've prayed to make it through to the finish line will all add up to what has become the process of your education.

The ending is the beginning. This chapter of your schooling may well be over, but the education of life has just begun. It will seek not only your mind but also your heart and your spirit. It will ask you to make choices you've never even considered before. It will force you to discover where the old you ends and the new you begins. This education will require you to remain grounded in your faith, so hold on to your mortarboard, because the ride will be picking up speed from here.

Continuing Education

For I can do everything with the help of Christ
who gives me the strength I need.

Philippians 4:13

The Starting Point

Starting something new is exciting! You create a dream for what's in front of you. You create yourself in a new way, discarding things that you know didn't work for you before, and trying new directions.

Every dream has a starting point, and it's up to you to decide not only when to start but also where to start and even how to start again if need be. What you may experience is that there was no straight line to get you from the starting point to your dream. What might be there is a yellow brick road, a road to Damascus, a wilderness path, or a Red Sea to cross.

Once you and God have set your compass point, let Him guide your steps and help you over, around, and through the seeming obstacles. Sometimes it will seem like starting over. Maybe it is, or maybe you'll just be shifting gears on the focus so you hit your target more directly.

Let the beginning be exciting! Let the journey build your character, your endurance, and your ability to receive the dream set before you. It's always a good day to get started.

Continuing Education

We...rejoice in our sufferings, because we know that suffering produces perseverance; perseverance, character; and character, hope. And hope does not disappoint us, because God has poured out his love into our hearts by the Holy Spirit.

Romans 5:3–5 NIV

There's a Time for Everything

The old cliché that says, "Timing is everything," contains a certain measure of truth. You may have wished for graduation day to come a lot sooner, or you may be slightly dreading the moment that a diploma is placed in your hand. With that diploma comes the expectation of those around you that now you will be even more responsible.

God works according to His timing and will challenge you to be wise in the things you do each day. You live in a world that will demand your time, and unlike some resources, you'll find time is not renewable. In fact, the reality is, you don't even know how much time you will get to spend. This time of graduation is quickly becoming your yesterday. Your new goals are your tomorrow. Today is the treasured moment you have to live. What will you do with your time today—for God, for others, and for yourself? Let this be a guiding question as you begin each day.

Continuing Education

There is a time for everything, a season for every activity under heaven. A time to be born and a time to die. A time to plant and a time to harvest. A time to kill and a time to heal. A time to tear down and a time to rebuild.

Ecclesiastes 3:1-3

Hats Off to You!

Graduation caps, those square black boards with tassels—that rarely fit anyone's head with ease—are the standard of most official ceremonies. They are a "different" kind of hat, and from now on, you're going to be wearing a lot of different hats. You may not particularly like the shape of this hat, or its color, or the way it looks on you, but that doesn't matter in the long run. What matters is what it represents, and what it stands for makes every wearer beautiful.

As you go out into the world and try on new hats and new ideas and new directions, it will be important for you to know what you stand for. You will have to answer the question Joshua threw out to his people centuries ago when he asked if they would choose today to serve the Lord. The world will ask you the same question. As Joshua said, "If you don't want to serve the Lord, you must choose for yourselves today whom you will serve" (Joshua 24:15 NCV).

May you continue to serve the Lord no matter what hat you wear or where life takes you. Hats off to you as you begin the journey anew.

Continuing Education

"As for me and my family, we will serve the Lord."

Joshua 24:15

Get Ready, Get Set, Be Still!

Now that you're all fired up to get out there and begin your new life adventure, take a moment to stop and look around. See where you are and how far you've come in this short time. Think about where you want to go and know that whatever your goals may be, there are a number of roads to help you get there. Quiet your dreams a moment and be still. Listen for the voice that has always been your teacher and wants your ultimate good more than anything in the world. Listen to the One who will always direct your steps.

Meister Eckhart said, "The very best and highest attainment in this life is to remain still and let God act and speak in you." As the days and years unfold before you, remember that whatever road you walk, you need to stop now and then and just wait on the Lord. At every turn, He will be there to renew your strength and guide your steps. Now, get ready, get set, and get going!

❀ ❀

Continuing Education

"Be silent, and know that I am God!
I will be honored by every nation.
I will be honored throughout the world."

Psalm 46:10

Back to Square One

Perhaps one reason that a graduation cap is square is because it reminds you that you're about to begin a new square on the game of life, a whole new direction on your path. In some ways, it will be square one. The good news is that it's square one on the next horizon, the next level up, the one that was once a goal to achieve. You've achieved. That means no matter where you are starting, you can achieve again. It's just a matter of believing that each step you take is carrying you closer to your dream.

Remember, you just have one real goal and that is to do a work that is pleasing to the Lord. He will go before you to lead the way, beside you to comfort you on the journey, and behind you to protect your well-being. So do as Goethe said when he wrote this great poem:

What you can do, or dream you can, begin it.
Boldness has genius, power, and magic in it.
Only engage, and then the mind grows heated;
Begin it and the task will be completed.

Continuing Education
In all the work you are doing, work the best you can.
Work as if you were doing it for the Lord, not for people.
Remember that you will receive your reward from the Lord,
which he promised to his people.

Colossians 3:23–24 NCV

It's Only the Beginning

When you were a child, you started new things with reckless abandon. You believed that anything was possible and that you could do everything. If you wanted to paint, you just needed a brush; if you wanted to sing, you just started the music; and if you wanted to know more, you simply asked questions.

As you start out on your new journey, begin with this idea: With God all things are possible! With God you can move mountains. With God you can paint like Van Gogh, sing like Frank Sinatra, and discover the secrets of the universe.

Ivy Baker Priest once said that "the world is round and the place which may seem like the end may also be the beginning." How exciting! You're at the beginning of all that is possible. Go with God and make your mark in the world!

Continuing Education

Jesus looked at them intently and said,
"Humanly speaking, it is impossible.
But with God everything is possible."
Matthew 19:26

BEING YOURSELF

THE POTTER AND THE CLAY

You've spent years now being molded and shaped, packed down, and started over. You've gone through a metamorphosis of all sorts as you've come to see yourself in new ways.

The next years of your life will continue the process. Those who elect to remold your thinking or redirect your purpose may change in levels of influence, but they'll all be there. It will be important for you to remember each day who the true Potter is. Isaiah 64:8 says this: "And yet, LORD, you are our Father. We are the clay, and you are the potter. We are all formed by your hand."

As you go forward into the next years of your life, remember whose you really are. Remember where to go for help when you're feeling fragile and uncertain. Your Father will hold you in His hand and shape you according to His will and purpose as long as you are willing to let Him.

CONTINUING EDUCATION

*For since the world began, no ear has heard, and no eye has seen
a God like you, who works for those who wait for him!
You welcome those who cheerfully do good, who follow godly ways.*

ISAIAH 64:4–5

The Courage to Be Yourself

M ost of your life, you've trained yourself to fit in. You've been someone's child, learning the values and the culture of your own home. You've learned the rules according to how you were taught them, and you've been, to some degree, comfortable there.

As you went through school, you also learned to fit into groups that you identified with or enjoyed for a variety of reasons. You played a sport, you joined the debate team, or you were part of the student council.

Now things are different. E. E. Cummings said, "It takes courage to grow up and become who you really are." You're here. It's a new crossroads. You'll take with you the precious things you learned at home, or at school, or in your church group that helped to mold the person you are as you graduate, but now you're on the path of your own discovery. Now you must find your own truth. It's okay, though; God will walk with you every step of the way.

❖ ❖

Continuing Education

Jesus said. . . "If you continue to obey my teaching,
you are truly my followers. Then you will know the truth,
and the truth will make you free."

John 8:31–32 NCV

Be True to Yourself

Though you might recognize the wisdom in the idea of being true to yourself, you may yet wonder, *Who am I? What do I really think? What is my self?* If so, you're not alone, but now is a good time to begin really knowing about you.

Who you are and who you will become are your gifts to the world. The trick in this discovery is that the earlier your truth becomes known, the quicker you can get on your ordained path and manifest those gifts. James Barrie once said, "The life of every one is a diary in which he means to write one story, and writes another." This is your time to begin writing your story. Make it the one that you meant to write.

God already is there ahead of you waiting to help you create your very best self. Start today and get to know someone really special—you!

Continuing Education

I could have no greater joy than to hear that my children live in the truth.

3 John 4

Be Original

You are the only you that will ever exist. You are not a copy of anyone else. You are God's design, and He created you as an original. That makes you unique in the world and precious to all those around you.

Sometimes education can be a process of taking away our originality, working hard to fuse us into the mold of sameness, of being like everyone else. You might even remember the painful experiences you had in junior high school of trying to be like everyone else so that you could fit in.

The good news is that God wants your unique contribution. Sure, you have to follow some of the cultural rules and norms to coexist with the rest of the world, but you don't have to lower your voice. Now it's time to rise up and be counted. Judy Garland once said, "Always be a first-rate version of yourself, instead of a second-rate version of somebody else."

Go on, be an original. It's your calling!

CONTINUING EDUCATION

Whatever is true, whatever is noble, whatever is right, whatever is pure, whatever is lovely, whatever is admirable—if anything is excellent or praiseworthy—think about such things. Whatever you have learned or received or heard from me, or seen in me— put it into practice. And the God of peace will be with you.

PHILIPPIANS 4:8–9 NIV

WHAT TO BE

As you step out into the world, hundreds of voices will gravitate toward you, shouting in your ear, "Come this way! Go that way! Here's the answer!" As you tune in to those voices, dismissing some and embracing others, you'll still come back to the nagging voice that asks, *What should I be?*

Charles Spurgeon suggests that you "be dogmatically true, obstinately holy, immovably honest, desperately kind, and fixedly upright." That sounds like a worthy goal to have.

- Dogmatically true? You will never compromise your truth.
- Obstinately holy? You will never be willing to give up your idea of holiness.
- Immovably honest? You will do all things with integrity.
- Desperately kind? You will seek to be kind at every turn.
- Fixedly upright? You will seek after God's righteousness with total courage and resolve.

These are indeed noble attributes. Today, take a look at them and put your name at the beginning of each phrase. Ask yourself if this is what you truly want to be. If it is, you have a place to start and a lifetime of discovery ahead of you.

CONTINUING EDUCATION

What does the LORD require of you? To act justly and to love mercy and to walk humbly with your God.

MICAH 6:8 NIV

What to Do

Being and doing may seem like similar things until you start to see that one is a system of understanding and one is a system of action. Once you know more accurately who you are, it is left then to discover what you will do with that information, how you will put your understanding into action.

John Wesley offered some insight into what we ought to do in the following:

> *Do all the good you can*
> *By all the means you can*
> *In all the ways you can*
> *In all the places you can*
> *To all the people you can*
> *As long as ever you can.*

The two words that really draw attention are "you can," which means that doing good in every way possible is a valid aspiration and regardless of your intelligence, your education, your life status, or your circumstances, you *can* do good forever.

CONTINUING EDUCATION

"Love your enemies, do good to them,
and lend to them without expecting to get anything back.
Then your reward will be great,
and you will be [children] of the Most High."

LUKE 6:35 NIV

What Do You See in the Mirror?

Before you go out today, spend a few moments in front of your mirror and be willing to see who you are. Once you get past the color of your eyes and the way your hair is not quite cooperating today, what else do you see?

Do you see the person that you want God to see today? Are you reflecting Him in the things you think and the places you go? Will you carry His light in your heart and in your spirit as you walk down the street or do business or go to school?

If you don't see Him as you look in your mirror, stop a moment. Put down the hairbrush, and call Him. Say, *Lord, help me become the person You want me to be. Help me reflect You to others. Help me to carry Your spirit of love and joy and kindness and goodness each place I go. Let every appointment I have today be a divine appointment so that each one who comes into the presence of my life comes into the presence of Your light. Amen.*

When you look back in the mirror, you may just see someone even more beautiful looking back at you.

Continuing Education
Be kind and compassionate to one another,
forgiving each other, just as in Christ God forgave you.
Ephesians 4:32 niv

CHANGE

WHY CHANGE?

You've spent most of your life like a chameleon changing your colors to fit the surroundings. At home you tried to be the dutiful child, the one who made your family proud. At school you were a good student and a good friend and socially active. At church you were thoughtful and loving and participated in events for the good of the group.

Here you stand on the precipice of change. All the colors you've worn before may integrate into your new surroundings just fine, but some things just won't fit the same way. Some things will ask you to become new.

New players will enter the picture, telling you your colors aren't just right, your look doesn't quite work, and your thinking doesn't quite match. Only you will be able to determine whether you believe changes need to be effected or not. Only you will know yourself well enough to be able to say out loud that you do need to change or you don't need to change.

The whole difference is that now, you must make those decisions based on all that is behind you and all that you still hope to achieve in front of you. You have deep roots in God, your family, your friends, and your interests. As you branch out, as you stretch and grow, draw near to your unchanging Father in heaven for strength and support.

CONTINUING EDUCATION

In his heart a man plans his course,
but the LORD determines his steps.

PROVERBS 16:9 NIV

YOUR SERENITY PRAYER

You know the Serenity Prayer as the one by Reinhold Niebhur. It says this: "God, grant me the serenity to accept the things I cannot change, the courage to change the things I can, and the wisdom to know the difference."

A more personal version goes, "God grant me the serenity to accept the people I cannot change, the courage to change the one I can, and the wisdom to know it's me."

Many things will happen in your life that you cannot change. Most will not be in your control. Wisdom comes from learning to keep your eyes on the One who is in control. He will be your source of unending grace and help you rise again when you need help to rise, and courage when you've lost your way.

Chaos will continue to flow around you, but the peace of God surpasses all understanding and will hold you tightly in the midst of any change that comes your way.

CONTINUING EDUCATION

Don't worry about anything; instead, pray about everything. Tell God what you need, and thank him for all he has done. If you do this, you will experience God's peace, which is far more wonderful than the human mind can understand.

PHILIPPIANS 4:6–7

Don't Get Too Comfortable

Most of us won't actively seek change. We won't get up each morning and make it our determination to be different by the end of the day. In fact most of us will say we're quite happy the way things are and we don't really need anything new to come our way.

St. Augustine recognized that what most of us need is a slight feeling of discomfort if we're actually going to look for change in our lives. He said, "If you would attain to what you are not yet, you must always be displeased by what you are. For where you are pleased with yourself, there you have remained. Keep adding, keep walking, and keep advancing."

Today is a new day. Are you totally pleased with your life as it is, or is there something that you could strive for— something you could add that would help you discover even more of what God designed you to be? Go after it, "keep adding, keep walking, and keep advancing"!

❖ ❖

Continuing Education

Grow in the special favor and knowledge of our Lord and Savior Jesus Christ.

2 Peter 3:18

Be the Change

Gandhi said you should "be the change you want to see in the world."

Be the change? How can you be the change?

God put it another way to Abraham. In Genesis 12:2 (NIV) we read, "I will make you into a great nation and I will bless you; I will make your name great, and you will be a blessing."

God may not be calling you to make your name great, but He still calls each of us to be a blessing to the world. Be the change. Be the blessing. If those around you are blessed by the things you do, the beliefs you stand for, and the love you share, then you are effecting change in their lives.

We live in a world that is hungry for blessing. Everyone you meet is fighting some kind of battle and your smile, your kind word, your hand of friendship will make a difference in their day and will change how they see things. You can be the change. You can bless those around you.

Abraham was blessed to be a blessing and so are you.

Continuing Education

"May the LORD bless you and protect you.
May the LORD smile on you and be gracious to you.
May the LORD show you his favor and give you his peace."

NUMBERS 6:24–26

GAME OVER; CHOOSE AGAIN!

Every day you have a new opportunity to create better choices, dream new dreams, and establish the direction of your life. That is the gift of God with each new sunrise, and only you determine whether you accept that gift or not. What happened yesterday, whether it brought extraordinary achievement or abysmal failure, is just part of your life journey. What happens today comes from the choices you have to make.

The good news and the bad news about choices is that ultimately they are something you have to own. You are responsible for them. When you've made an unfortunate choice, you need to forgive yourself as quickly as possible and get on to a new choice. Press the buzzer, thank you for playing, game over, and go on because there are a lot more choices to be made.

God is with you in your choices. He knows the desires of your heart and will help you establish your true direction as long as you let Him have control of your game plan. He wants you to win. Remember to include Him in any choice you make today.

CONTINUING EDUCATION

Don't let anyone think less of you because you are young.
Be an example to all believers in what you teach,
in the way you live, in your love, your faith, and your purity.
1 TIMOTHY 4:12

THE HEART OF DECISIONS

The world today often says that nothing we do is really "right" or "wrong," it's just part of the lessons we have to learn. Though we might be able to agree with that idea in some measure, we all know when we've actually made a wrong choice over a right choice. Usually a wrong choice will send a whole bunch of warning flags, sirens, whistles, and anything else it can to let us know we should rethink what we're doing. If you don't get an immediate thump on the head from Jiminy Cricket, then perhaps you've innocently made a wrong choice, but we're talking about something else here.

Erich Fromm said this about choices: "Our capacity to choose changes constantly with our practice of life. The longer we continue to make the wrong decisions, the more our heart hardens; the more often we make the right decisions, the more our heart softens or better, perhaps, comes alive."

Let your heart, your conscience, and the Holy Spirit guide you in all your decisions. Your best will "come alive" more often.

CONTINUING EDUCATION

We are the people he watches over, the sheep under his care.
Oh, that you would listen to his voice today!
The LORD says, "Don't harden your hearts."

PSALM 95:7–8

"Choice-a-phobia"

You have a lot of choices to make every single day—from what to wear to how to spend your free time to how to spend your money. Some choices are easy, and you win regardless of what you decide. In that regard, chocolate is always a good choice!

Other times, it seems like you lose no matter what you decide. You lose your job, or you lose that great paper you stored on your computer, or you lose your best friend. There are days when you can be almost afraid to make a choice. You become like Tevia in *Fiddler on the Roof*. You find yourself going, "On one hand, I could do this, but. . .on the other hand. . ." and then no choice can be made.

Theodore Roosevelt said, "In any moment of decision, the best thing you can do is the right thing, the next best thing is the wrong thing, and the worst thing you can do is nothing."

It's certainly not easy to always make good choices. The more you invite God's help with choices you have to make, the greater will be your sense of peace in any actions you take. Choose to share your choices with Him.

❖❖❖❖❖❖❖❖❖❖❖❖❖❖❖❖❖❖❖❖❖❖❖❖❖❖❖❖❖❖❖❖❖❖❖❖

Continuing Education

Humble yourselves, therefore, under God's mighty hand,
that he may lift you up in due time.
Cast all your anxiety on him because he cares for you.

1 Peter 5:6–7 NIV

THE ART OF CHOICE

According to André Gide, "Art is a collaboration between God and the artist, and the less the artist does the better."

The canvas of your life is before you, and each choice you make will add a stroke of genius or a blot of despair, but when your life is finished, you'll have a beautiful illustration of your life choices. How much of it reflects your true colors may depend largely on what part of it you left in God's hand. His design for you was set long before you were born.

Collaborate with Him today and let the Master paint a new day for you, bright with hope and joy and all that He would give to create beauty in all you do.

Give expression to your choices through His hand.

CONTINUING EDUCATION

When I consider your heavens, the work of your fingers,
the moon and the stars, which you have set in place,
what is man that you are mindful of him,
the son of man that you care for him?

PSALM 8:3–4 NIV

QUESTIONING
OUR CHOICES

When you've made choices, sometimes you look back and try to understand what you were thinking at the time that led you to choose the direction you did. That can be a worthwhile exercise as long as you're not dwelling on a wish that you had somehow taken a different path.

When choices come before you, whether they are moral or spiritual or full of fun, you might take a moment to question your responses. Rudyard Kipling put it rather cleverly in this short poem:

> *I keep six honest serving men*
> *(They taught me all I knew);*
> *Their names are What and Why and When,*
> *And How and Where and Who.*

If the results of your choices make a difference to you, then looking at the questions first might be God's way of keeping you honest about what you choose.

Choices are not flat. They have a lot of angles, and your questions will help you see the answers you seek more clearly.

CONTINUING EDUCATION

Godliness helps people all through life.

PROVERBS 13:6

COURAGE

SUPERHEROES

Superheroes always show up at just the right moment. They win every battle, and they're never afraid of anything no matter how big it is. It's no wonder that we perpetuate their existence and in some ways even wish they were real.

Superheroes do exist, though. They exist in you every time you're there to help someone in need. Every time you pray for the good of someone else. Every time you go out of your way to do someone a favor. You're a hero to someone when you give your time, your heart, and your helping hands to make sure a good work is done.

We don't always think of the everyday things as ones that require courage, but sometimes they do. Getting over the fears of achieving your dreams takes a special kind of courage. Persevering when the odds don't seem to be in your favor takes courage. Following your heart when no one else seems to support your dreams takes courage.

Dorothy Bernard said that "courage is fear that has said its prayers." Keep saying your prayers and have the courage to become all that God meant for you to be.

CONTINUING EDUCATION

"The good [person] brings good things out of the good stored up in his heart."

LUKE 6:45 NIV

The Courage to Stand. . .or Sit

We often credit the one who stands up in a group and expresses a persuasive opinion as being courageous. But sometimes real courage is not about speaking up; sometimes it's about not speaking at all. What happens when we're not speaking?

We're listening. Did you ever notice that when you make a decision to really listen to others, you discover very quickly the differences between those who simply seem to have something important to contribute, those who really do have something important to say, and those who just talk to hear themselves talk? While all that's going on, who's really listening?

George Eliot said, "Blessed is the [one] who, having nothing to say, abstains from giving wordy evidence of the fact." Being willing to speak up is one thing, but having the courage to be silent is quite another. Both have their consequences and rewards.

Have the courage to keep a few thoughts to yourself today.

Continuing Education

Even fools are thought to be wise when they keep silent;
when they keep their mouths shut, they seem intelligent.

Proverbs 17:28

The Little Engine of Courage

You probably remember the story of the little engine who was not so sure he could get up the mountain, but he talked to himself and just kept saying, "I think I can, I think I can."

Your life will have lots of moments when you won't be entirely sure you can scale the obstacles before you. Maybe you wondered if you could even get to graduation. Well, you're here and now you know you can.

Let that information lead the way as you move into new situations that require a little more courage than you think you have or a little more work than you've had to do before. It takes courage to begin something new, to face changes, and to move forward. It takes determination and persistence to keep moving up mountains that seem incredibly high.

Remind yourself today that whatever you have to attempt that might seem a little too hard is not impossible. Keep your eyes on Jesus and move toward the goal, and you will make it to the top.

Repeat this phrase: "I can do it, I can do it, I can do it—because God is with me."

Continuing Education

I can do everything through him who gives me strength.

PHILIPPIANS 4:13 NIV

EFFORT

Triumph:
The Try-Plus-"Umph" Combo

It takes a certain amount of courage to try anything new. Whether you're trying a different hairstyle or giving a speech for the first time, it's daunting. Trying things means that sometimes you'll be greatly successful and other times you'll be miserably disappointed.

One of the great "umphs"—if we could coin a word here—is prayer. Every try and every trial could use the umph of prayer to help you see your way through it or even to help you understand if you should do it in the first place.

Whenever you're going to put effort into something new or even something you've done before, the greatest triumph will come if you've asked for God's help along the way. Your success will be sweeter if it's based on knowing it was something your Creator wanted for you.

May your triumph today give you the courage to try even harder tomorrow.

Continuing Education

Make level paths for your feet and take only ways that are firm.
Proverbs 4:26 NIV

Effort Comes with an Eraser

Erasers may become obsolete. Elementary schools are becoming so well equipped with computers that we may one day cease to actually teach people to write letters on a piece of paper. In fact, paper itself seems to be going the way of chalk and slates. Our methods keep changing, but our effort doesn't.

Even if you're a perfectionist, you can't hit every perfect key or write every perfect word, and so you head for an eraser, or the white correction fluid, or the grammar checker.

If you could erase the way you spoke thoughtlessly to your friend, or "whiteout" the report you did at the last minute, you probably would. Sometimes you even have to erase an old idea to make room for a new one.

You can fix most of your efforts, but not all of them. Fortunately, God knew you couldn't fix the mistakes, sins, and things you do that you don't even like to admit. He took it upon Himself to provide the correction fluid for His own ledger. He erased those things you've confessed and asked forgiveness for. He did it all through Jesus Christ.

Each day, He gives you a clean slate to start again. What will you write on yours today?

Continuing Education

Those who become Christians become new persons.
They are not the same anymore, for the old life is gone.
A new life has begun!

2 Corinthians 5:17

It All Takes Work

S am Ewing somewhat humorously claimed this about effort: "Hard work spotlights the character of people; some turn up their sleeves, some turn up their noses, and some don't turn up at all."

We may smile at this, but all of us are in there somewhere, depending on what the job is. When you love the idea of a particular project, you get fired up, focused, and put everything you've got into your work. You work late, get up enthusiastic the next day, and can hardly wait to get at it again.

When the job is one you don't believe in or don't care to do, you may turn up your nose in some way. You're too busy to worry about the homeless campaign at church or to make a casserole for that family down the street. It's too much effort.

Other things just don't turn up on your agenda. Work, like everything else, though, is a matter of attitude and respect for what you're doing, regardless of whether you agree with all that must be done or not.

Where will you turn up today? The Lord always needs your best effort.

❀ ❀

CONTINUING EDUCATION

All a [person's] ways seem innocent to him,
but motives are weighed by the LORD.

PROVERBS 16:2 NIV

BECOMING A GREAT STREET SWEEPER

It's probably not your current goal to be a Wal-Mart greeter or a city street cleaner. After all, you've just graduated, and you've got the whole world waiting to see what you're going to become. Well, what you become is not nearly as important as who you are in the process of "becoming."

The people you graduated with and those in graduation classes from around the country and around the world all have the same choices. You might be heading to Harvard or a local community college, or maybe you're going to work in a family business or start a career at Wendy's. You can impress as many people as you want in any field you choose, but you will impress God in just one way.

When your heart leads according to God's will and purpose, your plans will succeed. Martin Luther King, Jr. said, "If a man is called a street sweeper, he should sweep streets even as Michelangelo painted, or Beethoven composed music, or Shakespeare wrote poetry. He should sweep streets so well that all the hosts of heaven and earth will pause to say, 'Here lived a great street sweeper who did his job well.'"

Do your job well, whatever it is.

CONTINUING EDUCATION

Work hard and cheerfully at whatever you do, as though you were working for the Lord rather than for people.

COLOSSIANS 3:23

THE CAT ATE MY HOMEWORK

Some people are gifted at giving reasons for why they weren't able to accomplish something. If you think back to when you were younger, you probably can even attach a name of someone who always had the most amazing excuses for why they were behind or didn't have their homework done or were out the day before.

In the adult world, some remain faithful to the creative excuse. They tell the boss they were ill, or their car ran out of gas on the way to work, or on and on and on.

You will be faced with temptations to offer excuses for doing less than was expected of you. You can rely on the fact that the cat ate your homework, even if you don't have a cat, or you can offer something that may speak more highly of you. You can offer to get the job done and stay late to do it if you have to. You can own and be responsible for your actions.

Someone once said that people stop looking for work once they find a job. Value yourself so much that you always produce a great effort and leave the excuses to someone with a dog.

CONTINUING EDUCATION

"Now, however, they have no excuse for their sin."
JOHN 15:22 NIV

Exercising Excuses

Too many people confine their exercise to jumping to conclusions, running up bills, stretching the truth, bending over backward, lying down on the job, sidestepping responsibility, and pushing their luck."

You may not buy into the anonymous quote above, but it might be a good idea to arm yourself with some new options so you don't even climb on the excuse treadmill. If you walk around with an idea for a while, you may not have to jump to conclusions.

If you balance your checkbook and count your blessings, you won't be as inclined to run up your bills. More flexible spending may cause you to stretch the truth about how that happened and then you'll be bending over backward to make up the deficit and get things to feel good again.

Of course, having an attitude of joy in contributing to your work so that you're a stand-up kind of person will never see you lying down on the job or sidestepping responsibility.

Pumping some iron into your prayer life will keep you from pushing your luck, and all of this together helps you run the race toward the good life God intended for you.

Continuing Education

Let us run with endurance the race that God has set before us.

Hebrews 12:1

EXPLORING

EXPLORING

EXPLORING

W illiam Blake wrote a lovely poem that goes:

To see a World in a Grain of Sand
And a Heaven in a wild Flower,
Hold Infinity in the palm of your hand
And eternity in an hour.

How much do you see? How much of all that God has given you do you cherish, praise Him for, or develop further? Blake's poem has hundreds of interpretations, but the one you might consider is the one that asks you to see more clearly. The one that suggests that every day, every moment, you're on an adventure, and God wants you to explore the landscape, the heart, and the soul of each thing you do.

Sip a glass of water, pick a flower, watch a bird as it chirps outside, and consider what God has done. You are a part of spaceship Earth, and He wants you to see today everything He's put in your hand. Use what He's given you to His glory.

❈ ❈

CONTINUING EDUCATION

"Blessed are your eyes because they see, and your ears because they hear. For I tell you the truth, many prophets and righteous men longed to see what you see but did not see it, and to hear what you hear but did not hear it."

MATTHEW 13:16-17 NIV

GETTING ON THE RIGHT TRACK

Graduation means you've accomplished something big and important, and you're really on the right track for getting your life moving in a great direction. Will Rogers reminded us that "even if you're on the right track, you'll get run over if you just sit there."

No doubt, you don't have any intention of just resting on your laurels, and it's even a good idea to take a deep breath before you head back out there to get on the new course. Just keep checking every now and then to see if you're still on track. You may discover that the world is one huge train station and there are tracks leading to almost anywhere, and some even lead to nowhere.

Your track is important to God, and He wants to travel with you all along the way. Before you move forward with a whole head of steam, check in with the Conductor and see just where you might find the best ticket to ride. Staying on track is a whole lot easier than fixing the course later on.

CONTINUING EDUCATION

Be strong and steady, always enthusiastic about the Lord's work,
for you know that nothing you do for the Lord is ever useless.

1 CORINTHIANS 15:58

FAILURE

What Is Failure?

Failure doesn't mean that you are a failure; it does mean you haven't yet succeeded.

Inventors and artists and writers and scientists all know what it's like to have their ideas rejected, their life work turned down, and their goals thwarted. Some may deem these things to be failures, but others took these rejections as challenges that only required further opportunity for success to happen.

How you choose to see those disappointments—that will surely come your way—will make the difference between failure and success, challenge and opportunity, no and yes. You have it in your hand to make that kind of choice.

Can you take the attitude of a scientist who tried a thousand times to create his dream and did not do so until the one thousand and first try? Can you receive rejection after rejection like Theodore Geisel did before he became the genius known as Dr. Seuss? Your attitude toward whatever you create defeats your cause or gives it wings. It's all up to you. What will you choose?

Continuing Education

"For I know the plans I have for you," says the LORD.
"They are plans for good and not for disaster,
to give you a future and a hope."
JEREMIAH 29:11

FAILURE AND ACCOMPLISHMENT

F ailure does not mean that you have accomplished nothing; it does mean you have learned something.

Your graduation means that you have reached a certain level of education that honors you for the work you've done so far and declares publicly that you have achieved a new degree of accomplishment. Schools help to define how you're doing in a very systematic way. If you do well, you go on to the next grade a year later, and if you don't, you take up the opportunity for that level of learning one more time.

When you are in the world beyond school, there are no easily identifiable markers to tell you whether you're passing or failing, making right choices or not. You may get some feedback from your job or from your peers, but it won't be that nice, clean measure of success you've been used to.

How will you know whether you're ready to move on to the next class, the next job, or the next opportunity? How will you measure your accomplishment? Perhaps the best way is to determine what you have to return to the Lord for the work you've done. What have you learned from your accomplishment?

CONTINUING EDUCATION

"His master replied, 'Well done, good and faithful servant!
You have been faithful with a few things;
I will put you in charge of many things.' "

MATTHEW 25:21 NIV

FAILURE AND FAITH

F ailure does not mean that you have been a fool; it does
mean you have a lot of faith.

You may recall at least one embarrassing moment when you stood red faced before one person or perhaps several. Maybe you forgot a line in the school play and it was painfully obvious, or you made the third out when your team needed a run desperately.

Sometimes when you've "failed" at something that you tried, you can feel foolish, especially if you really believed in what you were trying to do and went ahead when others didn't see the merit in it. You can imagine how difficult it must have been for the Wright brothers as they tried to build a plane, or even Noah as he tried to build an ark. Most of the people around probably said those efforts were crazy or foolish. Well, you already know what happened there.

What if you attempt something that others don't believe in, but you do?

Your attempt is a matter of sincere faith. If it took great faith to do it, it can never be counted as a failure. When was the last time you tried something that took great faith?

❖❖❖❖❖❖❖❖❖❖❖❖❖❖❖❖❖❖❖❖❖❖❖❖❖❖❖❖❖❖❖❖❖❖❖❖❖❖

CONTINUING EDUCATION

"Be strong and brave. Don't be afraid or discouraged."

1 CHRONICLES 22:13 NCV

FAILURE AND EFFORT

F ailure doesn't mean you don't have it; it does mean you have to do something in a different way.

You know the popular definition of insanity, the one where you do the same thing in the same way and expect a different result? Of course, if you never change your approach, getting a different result is going to be tough. In fact, getting a different result may not even be possible.

Where are you today? Are you thinking the exact same way you thought last week? Are you trying to accomplish something by using the same technique you've tried over and over? Each day is new. Each day brings you the chance to discover another approach to any issue you're trying to solve. You just need to be willing to try again.

Give yourself a break. Give yourself a chance to redefine the problem. Sing it, write it in poetry, talk about it with your cat, and then pray for new direction. When you're tired of trying the same old thing, God has new ideas. Send Him a message.

CONTINUING EDUCATION

This is the day that the Lord has made.
Let us rejoice and be glad today!

PSALM 118:24 NCV

FAILURE AND
LIFE GOALS

F ailure doesn't mean you've wasted your life; it does mean you have a reason to start fresh.

Somewhere in time, you started to define what you wanted to do with your life. You considered your skills and interests, and with the help of mentors and teachers, you headed for a goal. Graduation may signify you've reached that goal or that you're now on the way to completing that goal.

What happens when you encounter obstacles? Even more importantly, what happens if you achieve the goal but discover it was the wrong path for you? In our culture today, people change jobs on the average of seven times. Often they are not simply changing jobs but actually changing whole career paths. Does that mean they failed because they didn't keep going on the old track?

Of course not! It means they had a good reason to re-evaluate things and start something even better for themselves.

You may not be in a place of great change in your career path or job direction at this point, but some day you may be. How you see it will make all the difference in how quickly you succeed at something new. May God bless your life goals and dreams.

CONTINUING EDUCATION

I love the Lord, because he listens to my prayers for help.
He paid attention to me,
so I will call to him for help as long as I live.

PSALM 116:1–2 NCV

FAILURE AND "NOW OR NEVER"

F ailure doesn't mean you will never make it; it does mean it will take a little longer.

You understand how relative time is when you think back to when you were a kid waiting for Christmas—you couldn't sleep on Christmas Eve, and it seemed the morning would never come. Whenever you're waiting for something good to come into your life, time always seems to drag its feet.

When you're waiting for something like your dentist appointment, time seems to fly by, and you're back in that chair before you know it. If you've been waiting for an event in your life and it hasn't happened yet, it can feel like some kind of failing. Most people start to set timelines around things like when they assume they'll get a great job or get married or have kids. When you do that, those things can feel like traps you fall into when they don't happen on your schedule.

Today, give God your timeline. Reach right out there and hand Him your schedule and declare it His. That way, things will fall into place naturally according to His will and purpose for your life, and if you trust Him, you'll never have to worry about *when* something was supposed to take place again.

CONTINUING EDUCATION

And we know that God causes everything to work together for the good of those who love God and are called according to his purpose for them.

ROMANS 8:28

FAILURE AND GOD

F ailure does not mean God has abandoned you; it does mean God has a better way.

The darkest times in any human experience are those when it feels like God has left us. If you read Psalms, you'll find a lot of examples of those times when David questioned the Lord about why He was silent or where He was. Even Jesus seemed to ask God why He had forsaken Him at Gethsemane.

You may have those moments, too, when you wonder if God has simply walked away or if He was just too busy to see what you're going through. The answer is that God is just as close as ever, perhaps even more so, waiting for you to understand something important. He has a plan and a purpose for your life, and He wants you to achieve the goal that is set. Sometimes, to help you accomplish that goal, He redirects the steps so that you get there in a better way.

When the clouds are hanging low and you can't quite see what's ahead, just know that there's a light on for you, and that flame is eternal.

CONTINUING EDUCATION

Examine yourselves to see if your faith is really genuine. Test yourselves. If you cannot tell that Jesus Christ is among you, it means you have failed the test.

2 CORINTHIANS 13:5

FAITH AND REASON

John Donne said, "Reason is our soul's left hand, faith her right."

As a person with a strong intellect, you'll find it easy to reason things out most of the time. We tend to think of things as reasonable if we can understand the whys and wherefores. When we can examine the facts and determine the best course of action or create a favorable outcome using all the gifts God gave us, that seems reasonable.

We think someone is a reasonable person when they operate from a view that allows us to have an opinion or to share in the direction of things. Reasoning serves us well, and being reasonable people may serve us even better.

Looking at Donne's comment, however, reason is perhaps the weaker brother. Assuming for a moment that the right hand is dominant, faith becomes the stronger ally. When reason fails, faith comes into play.

Moments will come in your life when reason will utterly fail you. Your joy will be full as you realize that faith is your anchor, your stronghold in any storm, and your light in the deepest shadows of doubt. Rejoice in your faith.

CONTINUING EDUCATION

"Come now, let us reason together," says the LORD.

ISAIAH 1:18 NIV

Handle with Faith

Henry Ward Beecher once said, "Every tomorrow has two handles. We can take hold of it with the handle of anxiety or the handle of faith." Which handle do you want to hold on to?

The handle of anxiety is always there, ready to be picked up, never far from view, never hard to find. Each day presents challenges for the heart, the mind, or the soul. Each day gives you a choice.

Most of us pick up that anxiety handle as though it were an old friend. We hug it with some level of familiarity and actually have trouble giving it up should the handle of faith start to show itself.

Whatever you have to handle, give faith a chance. Pray for guidance with your concern and know that God is ready and able to handle anything with you. Pray, "Lord, I know that nothing will happen to me today that You and I can't handle."

Continuing Education

"Do not be discouraged,
for the LORD your God will be with you wherever you go."
Joshua 1:9 NIV

A Faith with Wings

Whenever an obstacle presents itself in my life, I've found it always helps to imagine myself as a little bird that can fly way above whatever is going on around me. As that little bird, I can gain a new perspective as I look upon the obstacle with clearer vision about how to move forward.

Life requires the faith to see ahead of where you are now, the belief that God is working with you to create a new plan and a hope for the future. Sometimes you'll have to give your faith wings so it can free you from doubt and worry and the things that slow you down in your efforts.

Sometimes you may just feel too weary to go on for the moment, and you'll need to rest in your faith, taking comfort that answers will come and new opportunities will present themselves. When you feel stuck and a bit too close to all that feels like it's caving in around you, remember to give your faith wings and fly above it for just a while. God will renew your strength and your spirit.

Continuing Education

But those who wait on the Lord will find new strength.
They will fly high on wings like eagles.
They will run and not grow weary.
They will walk and not faint.

Isaiah 40:31

THE FORT KNOX OF FAITH

I f you think of Fort Knox as the reservoir of resources in terms of gold and money that supports our economy and helps build our material and physical well-being, then your faith is the Fort Knox of your spirit. Your faith is what supports every area of your life. Therefore, you must make daily deposits of prayer and scripture to keep those reservoirs full.

B. C. Forbes said that "he who has faith has. . .an inward reservoir of courage, hope, confidence, calmness, and assuring trust that all will come out well—even though to the world it may appear to come out most badly."

Protecting, nurturing, and growing your faith is essential to your well-being both in this life and the next. Deposits into your bank account serve you well while you're here, but deposits into your faith account will serve you well for eternity. Be sure to strengthen your reserve every chance you get.

❊❊❊❊❊❊❊❊❊❊❊❊❊❊❊❊❊❊❊❊❊❊❊❊❊❊❊❊❊❊❊❊❊❊❊

CONTINUING EDUCATION

[Jesus said,] "I advise you to buy gold from me—gold that has been purified by fire. Then you will be rich. And also buy white garments so you will not be shamed by your nakedness. And buy ointment for your eyes so you will be able to see. I am the one who corrects and disciplines everyone I love."

REVELATION 3:18–19

Just a Little Faith

Sometimes when Jesus was trying to make a point with His disciples and they came up with the wrong answer or simply didn't get what He was talking about, He would comment about their "little faith."

On one such occasion, the disciples were complaining that they had forgotten to bring food to a big gathering where Jesus was teaching, and so they told Him of their concerns. He reminded them that they had fed over five thousand with a few loaves and fishes not so long ago and that they had fed four thousand on another occasion with seven loaves and few small fish. Had they already forgotten these things?

When you find yourself worrying over something as small as how to feed five thousand people—or maybe even five people—look at your faith quotient and see if its size is part of the difficulty. God's plan is always to give you more than you could even ask. Imagine if you had more than a little faith!

Remember, "A little faith will bring your soul to heaven, but a lot of faith will bring heaven to your soul."

Continuing Education

Jesus knew what they were thinking, so he said,
"You have so little faith!
Why are you worried about having no food?
Won't you ever understand?"

Matthew 16:8–9

INVISIBLE STAIRS

M artin Luther King, Jr., said, "Faith is taking the first step even when you don't see the whole staircase."

You may remember an Indiana Jones movie when he and his father were searching for the Holy Grail. At one point, the clue was about a man of faith, and the actor showed us how he stepped out in faith over a sheer cliff only to discover that once he took the step, the stairs were there—or in that case, the stones to step on.

Faith will ask you to move forward even before you see a way to get there. It will cause you to push through your fears, tune out the world, and listen only to the guidance of the Holy Spirit. When that happens, surrender. The steps you take will create the way for all that needs to be done.

Step out in faith, and you'll discover the foundation stone was set a long time ago to support you in your walk.

CONTINUING EDUCATION

*"You have made a wide path for my feet
to keep them from slipping."*

2 SAMUEL 22:37

Feed Your Faith

If you want to starve your fears, you have to feed your faith. How do you do that?

You can feed your faith a number of ways, and many of these ways need to become daily habits. Just as you feed your body, you need to feed your faith. Imagine if you were to feed your faith with three square meals a day. For breakfast, you might pour out your heart in prayer, strengthening your body with a large sprinkling of the Spirit's go power for the day. You'll really have eaten the breakfast of champions.

For lunch you might feast on the Word and give yourself a full portion to carry around in your knapsack as the day goes on. You'll be sandwiched in grace and mercy and peace, and you'll be energized to take on the world for the rest of the day.

At dinnertime, you'll want to renew your spirit by refreshing your heart and mind and soul by simply being still so that God can speak to you, offer you a generous serving of His love, and prepare you to rest in His care.

Feeding your soul, feasting on your faith, will rescue you from fear.

Memorize a favorite scripture for dessert.

Continuing Education

Let the words of Christ, in all their richness,
live in your hearts and make you wise.
Use his words to teach and counsel each other.

Colossians 3:16

FAMILY

Family Ties

You may be getting ready to go out into the world for the first time, seeking your own path, gaining higher knowledge, and finding out who you are apart from your family. All of that is important and part of what you were designed to do at this time in your life.

As you do that, though, remember that your family is not leaving you. They are still there for you, offering support, creating a space to come back to when you're ready to share your adventures. Desmond Tutu said, "You don't choose your family. They are God's gift to you, as you are to them."

Wherever you go in life and whatever you do, your family will always remain a "North Star." They will always be a compass point, a way back, even if it's simply to embrace the joy of days gone by. Keep your family close to your heart.

❖❖❖❖❖❖❖❖❖❖❖❖❖❖❖❖❖❖❖❖❖❖❖❖❖❖❖❖❖❖❖❖❖❖❖

Continuing Education

His name is the LORD—rejoice in his presence!
Father to the fatherless, defender of widows—this is God,
whose dwelling is holy. God places the lonely in families.

Psalm 68:4–6

You're Not Graduating
from the Family

A s you reach the graduation milestone, it's easy to think of it as a chance to get out on your own and leave behind the good, the bad, and the ugly of your family. If you come from Perfectville, you may have the one-in-a-million family that you couldn't imagine leaving behind. But if you're like most of us, there are things about your family dynamics that really encourage you to be getting out on your own.

Culturally, we live in all kinds of family situations. Whether you have a traditional nuclear family, a blended family, a single-parent family, an adopted family, or some other combination, those people are the ones who have devoted a great deal of time and energy to your well-being. Jane Howard said, "Call it a clan, call it a network, call it a tribe, or call it a family. Whatever you call it, whoever you are, you need one."

That pretty well sums it up. As John Donne once wrote, "No man is an island." We're all designed to be part of something, and however you structure family, yours is a blessed part of your support system. When you take the step to go out on your own, remember it doesn't mean that you need to totally leave your family support behind.

Continuing Education

*Carry each other's burdens,
and in this way you will fulfill the law of Christ.*

GALATIANS 6:2 NIV

WHO IS YOUR FAMILY?

As you move out into the world, you may discover some new definitions for *family*. You will find yourself involved with a lot of people who care about you and love you but who are not blood relatives. These people will become your family, as well. Your new "family" may come from your church group, your workplace, or some special-interest group.

Why do you think of them as family? You do because they provide those essential ingredients of support, kindness, interest, and love that you always need. You may have a mentor in college or in the workplace, or a spiritual teacher in a prayer group. These people are God's gifts to you, as well. Pearl Buck suggested that one mother and one father could never be enough to give us everything we need. We must create the world as our family so that we stay connected to each other.

When you see others as your family, you may understand what joy there is in service. God thinks of all of us as His family, and that is why He sent Jesus to serve us and to be served by us. Those things only happen by deep connection.

As you go out today, reconnect with your family, no matter where you find them.

CONTINUING EDUCATION

Whenever we have the opportunity,
we should do good to everyone,
especially to our Christian brothers and sisters.

GALATIANS 6:10

Family Education

One reason to deeply respect your family is that these people offered you your first instruction about yourself, the world, and how you might understand the things of God. From them, you learned how to take care of yourself, what some of the rules are, and even who you are.

Billy Graham said the "family was ordained by God before He established any other institutions, even before He established the church." That's a helpful insight as to how important your family is to God.

Your education started long before you went to day care or kindergarten. It started the moment you were born and you discovered that you were already in the arms of people who loved you and cared about you. Those people will always hold you in their hearts and in their arms. Even now, as they work to let go of you so that you can move forward and someday create your own family, they will hold tender memories of all they learned from you.

Carry in your heart all that you learned from them, as well.

Continuing Education

If any one does not provide for his relatives,
and especially for his own family,
he has disowned the faith and is worse than an unbeliever.

1 Timothy 5:8 RSV

FORGIVENESS

An Attitude of Forgiveness

P erhaps you may wonder at the topic of "forgiveness" being addressed in a book that hopes to motivate and inspire you as you move out into the world. Or perhaps you've already discovered the essential gift that forgiveness brings into each life.

Martin Luther King, Jr. said that "forgiveness is not an occasional act: It is an attitude."

The forgiveness attitude must be embraced, tutored, created, and educated like any other attitude or opinion you hold. The first one you must be willing to nurture, love, and forgive is yourself. Take those moments from the past that you have not yet forgiven, and let today be a new start.

You cannot change the past when you forgive, but you can change the future. As you pack up the things you want to take into your new life, spend a little time cleaning out and clearing up the things you don't want to take. Be forgiving to someone very special—you.

❈ ❈

Continuing Education

The LORD is like a father to his children,
tender and compassionate to those who fear him.
For he understands how weak we are; he knows we are only dust.
PSALM 103:13–14

Trespassers Will Be Forgiven

I t's always great to begin new things. Graduation is called "commencement" because it is the beginning of another stage in your life. It's the beginning of new dreams and hopes and discoveries.

Your relationship with God "commences" each day, as well. His mercies are new every morning. He always gives you an opportunity to begin with a new heart.

One part of the Lord's Prayer says, "Forgive us our trespasses as we forgive those who trespass against us." What is trespassing, anyway? One definition refers to *trespass* as "breaking a moral or social law." Another talks about causing an injury to someone or to their property or to their rights. All of us have trespassed against someone else at one time or another.

The Lord's Prayer reminds us that we must ask for forgiveness from God as we embrace the act of forgiving those who have trespassed against us. It's a new day! Anyone you have not forgiven from yesterday awaits your change of heart. God awaits your change of heart, as well. In His book, all "trespassers" are forgiven.

Continuing Education

Praise the LORD, I tell myself,
and never forget the good things he does for me.
He forgives all my sins and heals all my diseases.

PSALM 103:2–3

GRADUATE FROM GRUDGES

G raduation is an excellent time to take a little inventory and discover whether you're holding any old baggage from your high school or college days that may not serve you as you move into the world. Are you still harboring resentment for the kid who the got the part you wanted in the school play, or the one who always seemed to come out on top no matter what the situation was about?

Are you remembering the kid in grade school who teased you on the playground, and somehow you bought into it but never realized you didn't have to? Do you have a teacher who seemed unfair to you and didn't give you a much-deserved A, even when you worked hard for it? Whatever your example might be of old injuries from your school days, now is a good time to let them go.

Disappointment, injustice, and sadness all need to be left behind now. All those grudges need to be forgiven before you leave school. Those old weights will never serve you well. Let them stay as far from you as the east is from the west, and give yourself a chance to start fresh. You'll feel much better if you do.

CONTINUING EDUCATION

Disregarding [forgiving] another person's faults preserves love; telling about them separates close friends.

PROVERBS 17:9

Healthy Forgiveness

You're probably already very conscious of creating time for yourself to work out, eat right, and do the things that will keep you healthy. Good health really is key to your accomplishments. It gives you the necessary energy and drive to get things done.

Your emotional health is also key to what you accomplish, and part of that health comes from your ability to recognize the need to forgive and to be forgiven. Forgiving yourself on a daily basis is akin to the proverbial "apple a day." It will keep you strong.

Forgiving others lightens your heart and your spirit, restoring, renewing, and creating a space in your soul for blessings to abound. While you're working out today, or treading on a treadmill, or walking your dog at the park, consider those who might need a little forgiveness from you and bless them. Ask God for a way for your forgiveness health to be restored. It will cause blessings to flow.

Continuing Education

Then Peter came to Jesus and asked,
"Lord, when my fellow believer sins against me,
how many times must I forgive him?
Should I forgive him as many as seven times?"
Jesus answered, "I tell you, you must forgive him
more than seven times. You must forgive him even if
he does wrong to you seventy-seven times."

Matthew 18:21–22 NCV

FRIENDSHIP

The Giving Side of Friendship

Octavia Butler reminded us, "Sometimes being a friend is mastering the art of timing. There is a time for silence. A time to let go and allow people to hurl themselves into their own destiny. And a time to prepare to pick up the pieces when it's all over."

When you give time or energy or love to a friend, it doesn't always mean solving problems for them or having them solve yours. Sometimes it means trusting together that God has plans for your lives and will be with you in the silence or with you as you make an effort toward your goal. The outcome is not about winning or losing, in either achieving the goal or creating your friendships; the outcome is about giving your time and trusting God to be with you through it all.

Today as you spend time with friends, consider what it is you really choose to give in those relationships.

CONTINUING EDUCATION

There is a time for everything,
a season for every activity under heaven.

ECCLESIASTES 3:1

FOLLOW THE LEADER

R emember the game called "Follow the Leader"? In the game, someone is at the front of the line, and whatever motion they perform, you perform, as well. The point of the game is to not think for yourself.

School can feel like that. You're always following the guidelines of teachers or peers or parents. Now you must think for yourself, both following and leading in your school and work experiences and in your friendships.

Albert Camus gave us a thought to ponder concerning the best place to be when it comes to creating strong friendships.

> *Don't walk behind me,*
> *I may not lead.*
> *Don't walk in front of me,*
> *I may not follow.*
> *Just walk beside me and be my friend.*

Today, walk beside your friends, but keep following your leader, Jesus Christ.

CONTINUING EDUCATION

"You are my friends if you obey me."

JOHN 15:14

HOLDING UP THE LIGHT

Y ou may be discovering some new things about friendships now. They are not necessarily born by linking up with those who are most like you. Sometimes they are born by linking up with those who are willing to hold up a mirror so that you can see who you really are. Good friends will hold up a light for you so you can see your reflection more clearly.

It's important always to have good friends and trusted relationships. Albert Schweitzer illuminated real friendships in this quote: "Sometimes our light goes out but is blown into flame by another human being. Each of us owes deepest thanks to those who have rekindled that light."

You may have days when your own light is dim or your path wearying. On those days, you may find comfort in the kindness of a friend. Remember, too, that there is One who is always holding up the light for you. Jesus is not only the Light of the World, but He is indeed the Light of your very life.

Shine on today.

CONTINUING EDUCATION

A friend is always loyal,
and a brother is born to help in time of need.

PROVERBS 17:17

THE INSPIRATION OF FRIENDS

R alph Waldo Emerson said, "The glory of friendship is not the outstretched hand, nor the kindly smile, nor the joy of companionship; it is the spiritual inspiration that comes to one when he discovers that someone else believes in him and is willing to trust him with his friendship."

As with all relationships, we choose our friends for a variety of reasons. Sometimes we choose friends who we know we can count on—whatever life brings—to offer us solace or comfort. Sometimes we choose friends who make us laugh or cheer us up when the need arises. Other times, a friend serves a higher purpose.

We know that part of our faith in Jesus Christ and our desire for a friendship with Him has to do with knowing that He is always there for us, always desiring our best, and always hearing our cries for help. Some friends are like that in that they inspire us to become more than we would ever be without their help. They believe in us and know that we are called to live according to God's purpose.

When you cultivate those friends, you will know real joy indeed.

CONTINUING EDUCATION

A real friend sticks closer than a brother.

PROVERBS 18:24

GIVING

The Flint, the Sponge, and the Honeycomb

G ivers can be divided into three types: the flint, the sponge, and the honeycomb. Some givers are like a piece of flint—to get anything out of it, you must hammer it, and even then you may only get chips and sparks. This kind of giver may never light a fire in the world.

Some givers are like sponges. To get anything out of a sponge, you must squeeze it and squeeze it hard, because the more you squeeze a sponge, the more you get, at least until it runs dry. This kind of giver mostly soaks up the gifts of others.

Some givers, though, are like a honeycomb. A honeycomb just overflows with its sweetness, giving all it can. This is how God gives to us and how we should give in return.

Consider what kind of giver you are. Do others find a new spark of joy in your warmth, a taste of compassion in your kindness, or bask in the sweetness of your love?

✿✿✿✿✿✿✿✿✿✿✿✿✿✿✿✿✿✿✿✿✿✿✿✿✿✿✿✿✿✿✿✿✿✿✿

Continuing Education

For God loves the person who gives cheerfully.

2 Corinthians 9:7

THE MORE YOU GIVE,
THE MORE YOU LIVE

A n old poem goes like this:

Give strength, give thought, give deeds, give wealth;
Give love, give tears, and give yourself.
Give, give, be always giving,
Who gives not, is not living;
The more you give, the more you live.

When you give from the heart, you never run out of the energy to give more. Have you ever noticed that when you're caught up in something you're doing that makes you feel good, that feels effortless, you hardly feel like you gave anything to it at all? On the other hand, when you're made to do something that you can't put your heart into, the whole situation changes and it takes great work to accomplish it?

The real givers in the world do so without a need for recognition, without a thought to what they have given. They give the gifts of the heart. Consider not only what you might want to give to the world from your heart, but how you will give to the world. It is a difference worth recognizing.

CONTINUING EDUCATION

"Do for others as you would like them to do for you."

LUKE 6:31

GIVING AND GETTING

Winston Churchill gave us the wonderful adage "We make a living by what we get. We make a life by what we give."

Most of us are largely in a frenzy of getting. We have the poor impression that the one with the most toys wins the game. Our obsession with more and bigger and better makes us almost unaware that we already have more than most of the people in the known world.

If you're sleeping in a warm bed tonight after having a nice dinner and watching your favorite TV show, you're in the minority. You're living among the wealthy. You're part of the "getting" group.

Of course, the extremes are on either side of us, but every day be grateful for what you have already attained. Consider your attitude and your motivation for getting more. And once you've done all of that, ask yourself what you're willing to give to make it all possible.

Giving is its own reward.

CONTINUING EDUCATION

*"You should remember the words of the Lord Jesus:
'It is more blessed to give than to receive.'"*

ACTS 20:35

WHAT ARE YOU GIVING?

You are the Bible
The world is reading;
You are the gift
The world is needing—
All you do matters
For you are leading.

G iving is more than simply something we consciously do in the form of a gift or an answer to a test question. Giving is what happens when anyone observes us from afar or under a microscope. What we give off in the forms of truth and beliefs and commentary are the things that most of us unwittingly share with others. We are constantly giving an impression. We are always giving something of ourselves anytime we are present with others.

No matter where you go or what you do today, remember that you're giving someone an impression, not just of you, but also of themselves and of the God who lives in your soul.

God is the One who gives seed to the farmer and bread for food.
He will give you all the seed you need and make it grow so there
will be a great harvest from your goodness.

2 CORINTHIANS 9:10 NCV

GOALS

JUST DO IT!

The oft-quoted Nike slogan is simple and to the point. It's worth meditating on whether you're talking about running a race or getting to the next level of achievement or a job promotion. When it comes right down to it, there's no one else who can "just do it" like you can.

If you've been considering a new direction for your life and you've also found an obstacle to where you want to go, then maybe it's time to convince yourself to climb over, around, or through whatever the barriers are and just get yourself out there and get the job done. Just do it!

Brother Lawrence said, "All things are possible to him who believes, yet more to him who hopes, more still to him who loves, and most of all to him who practices and perseveres in these three virtues." Today is a good day to make things happen and to reach those goals of your heart and mind. Keep going—you can do it!

❈❈❈❈❈❈❈❈❈❈❈❈❈❈❈❈❈❈❈❈❈❈❈❈❈❈❈❈❈❈❈❈❈❈❈❈

CONTINUING EDUCATION

"All things are possible for the one who believes."
MARK 9:23 NCV

No Goals, No Glory!

The adage "If you aim at nothing, you'll hit it" reminds us how important it is to set attainable goals. Most students have goals already in mind when they first graduate. The question is, what happens when you either meet or move away from your first goal and have no idea where to go next?

How do you recapture them or set new goals? One of the best practices is to make a list of where you want to be in the next six months or six years. Give yourself steps to achieve those goals. When you're trying to lose weight, you start a goal-setting program for exercise, calorie intake, and rewards. You can do the same thing in other areas of your life, as well.

Define your goal and set your intention. Write down which parts of your goal are in your hands. Who are the people you know who might help you along the way? What skills do you possess to make your goal possible? What education do you still need?

Act on your goals. Simply writing down appropriate steps for weight loss won't get you to the goal. The work still remains to be done. The actions need to be taken.

Reward yourself. Give yourself simple rewards when you've completed steps toward your goals. If nothing else, you deserve a good chocolate brownie. Remember—no goals, no glory!

Continuing Education

So let us run the race that is before us and never give up.

Hebrews 12:1 NCV

GOALTENDING

T he goalie or the goaltender in a hockey game is the one who keeps a watchful eye on the area around the net anytime the puck gets close to a chance to cross the line and into the net. He has to be constantly alert, ready to fly toward the net and guard the goal at any moment.

You have goals that need protecting, as well. Sometimes others will not believe in your dreams, or they will feel that your timing isn't right, or that you should go a direction that feels more comfortable to them. Though those people in your life mean well, they may not have been called to do what you feel called to do, and therefore you must trust the Great Goaltender to be with you and help you watch out for and protect your goal.

B. C. Forbes put it this way: "History has demonstrated that the most notable winners usually encountered heartbreaking obstacles before they triumphed. They won because they refused to become discouraged by their defeats."

Whatever the obstacles are to your goals, know that God is on your side and that, alone, gives you the majority vote. Keep trying.

CONTINUING EDUCATION

People may make plans in their minds,
but the Lord decides what they will do.

PROVERBS 16:9 NCV

A Life of Purpose

Probably no one has done more to help us realize life has meaning and purpose than Rick Warren in *A Purpose Driven Life*.

Finding your purpose is one of the greatest goals you might have. Purpose is much more than a job or a career path; it's a calling, a reason for being.

Pastor Warren reminds us of Psalm 139 and confirms that God knew us before we were born. He had a plan for us that will carry on past our own generation and make a difference for all time.

This helps you see your goals from a new perspective. Now you have a mission and one that God ordained before you were even a bit of protoplasm. What you do with this time on earth is important to Him and to completing the work He needs to have done.

As you seek your own goals, continue to align with Him in prayer and seek His guidance and direction. The reward will be evident in the spirit in which you create your work and the joy that comes to all who are part of it with you.

Discover your purpose—it's important.

Continuing Education

For everything, absolutely everything, above and below, visible and invisible. . .everything got started in him and finds its purpose in him.

Colossians 1:16 msg

GOD

GOD CREATED YOU

C. H. Spurgeon said, "He who counts the stars and calls them by their names, is in no danger of forgetting His own children. He knows your case as thoroughly as if you were the only creature He ever made, or the only saint He ever loved."

God created you. He knows you and every aspect of you. His love for you is boundless, and His joy in you comes full circle each time you call Him into your life in prayer.

Whatever your plans are, your goals, your dreams. . .the One who already knows your choices is there beside you. Share your vision with Him so He can share His with you. It is the best way to achieve the true desires of your heart.

Today, know and believe that you are a child of God, created with love and destined to achieve great things for His glory.

✾✾✾✾✾✾✾✾✾✾✾✾✾✾✾✾✾✾✾✾✾✾✾✾✾✾✾✾✾✾✾✾✾✾✾

CONTINUING EDUCATION

I praise you because you made me in an amazing and wonderful way.
What you have done is wonderful. I know this very well.
You saw my bones being formed as I took shape
in my mother's body. . . . All the days planned for me
were written in your book before I was one day old.

PSALM 139:14–16 NCV

Your Will and God's Will

O ne of the things we all deal with is the power struggle between what we want to have happen, what we want to be in control of, and what we want God to be in control of. Glibly, we may say we want God to be in total control of our lives. In truth, He is.

The hard part is surrendering each new day to engaging His will with an open heart, ready to receive what He wants and knows is best for you.

Try to think of yourself as only existing in this moment in time to do God's will. You were in the mind of God long before you got to this planet. Therefore, you belong completely to God.

Since you already know where you belong, why not bask in the joy of what is already yours and praise the One who cares more for you than any human ever could?

Continuing Education

He came to the world that was his own,
but his own people did not accept him.
But to all who did accept him and believe in him
he gave the right to become children of God.

John 1:11-12 NCV

Your Way and God's Way

A s human beings we're always looking for a better way to do things. That's a worthy trait in us because certainly some of the "better ways" that have developed in the last hundred years have made our lives a lot more efficient and convenient. Looking to do things a better way, then, is a good thing.

When it comes to how we want to get things done, C. S. Lewis said there are two kinds of people: "There are those who say to God, 'Thy will be done,' and those to whom God says, 'All right, then, have it your way.'"

When you're trying to figure out which way to go today, which outcome would you prefer? You may not always be certain you want to do it God's way, but if it means God has to walk away so you can do it your way, it might be worth thinking it through again.

You may be able to "have it your way" at Burger King, but you may not actually want your way if it means you've lost *the* King.

CONTINUING EDUCATION

And this world is fading away, along with everything it craves. But if you do the will of God, you will live forever.

1 JOHN 2:17

What, You Worry?

As a general rule, people are worriers. Even good Christians worry. Mark Twain was known to have said near the end of his life, "I am an old man and have known a great many troubles, but most of them have never happened."

No matter how many times you prove the truth of that statement to yourself, five minutes after admitting that you believe your life is in God's hands, you start to worry about the next thing on your plate, just in case God isn't paying attention to you that day.

A lot of college students—and a lot of adults in general—find that worry will keep them up half the night. No doubt by the light of day, they discovered that things turned out better than they anticipated, but that didn't stop the worry. Mary C. Crowley put it in this context: "Every evening I turn my worries over to God. He's going to be up all night anyway."

Your worries don't have to keep you up all night. Believe that God has your life in His hand and that He cares for you so much that He holds every detail. Take worry out of your agenda for today.

Continuing Education

"So don't worry about tomorrow, for tomorrow will bring its own worries. Today's trouble is enough for today."

Matthew 6:34

What You Believe

When things are going along pretty well, you're probably like most of us in that you're feeling safe in God's care and able to give Him the credit for all the good that surrounds you. When things aren't going quite so well, you may also be like most of us if you begin to wonder what it is you actually do believe about God. Miguel de Unamuno tried to distinguish between a belief in the idea of God and a true belief in God: "Those who believe that they believe in God, but without passion in their hearts, without anguish in mind, without uncertainty, without doubt, without an element of despair even in their consolation, believe in the God idea, not God himself."

In other words, passion, emotion of any kind, uncertainty, and questioning are all part of the idea of what we believe in or about God. Believing in God is a much more direct path. You simply believe. No question.

The quest for God will always be with you, no matter how old you are or how successful you become. May your beliefs become stronger than your questions.

Continuing Education

How great is our Lord! His power is absolute!
His understanding is beyond comprehension!

Psalm 147:5

Hello, Where Are You?

Have you ever noticed how easy it is to hide from God? You know those times when you feel too busy, or you're doing something that you think as a human being is okay to do—but maybe not something you want to talk to God about. Maybe, like Adam and Eve, you're feeling rather vulnerable and don't want to come out to meet God in the clearing.

When those times occur, see if you can come face-to-face with yourself and be straight about what it is that's really going on. Why is this particular thing something that makes you want to hide in the bushes and hope the Lord is not walking by at just that moment?

It's always good to examine your motives and your heart and even the very acts that you're putting yourself through to determine if it feels like you'd be right before God.

If you're not sure, it might be good to spend a little time getting more acquainted. When God calls your name, you want to be right close by.

Continuing Education

Toward evening they heard the Lord God walking about in the garden, so they hid themselves among the trees. The Lord God called to Adam, "Where are you?"

GENESIS 3:8–9

The Good Earth and God

A s night turns to day, and waking dreams return, you're once again a guest of the planet Earth. Whether you live in the country or the city, you look out and find the same sun and the same sky protecting you overhead. The clean air fills your lungs, and you breathe in the life of all that's around you.

Rebecca Harding Davis wrote, "We are all of us from birth to death guests at a table which we did not spread. The sun, the earth, love, friends, our very breath are parts of the banquet. . . . Shall we think of the day as a chance to come nearer our Host, and to find out something of Him who has fed us for so long?"

As you rise to the new day, see if you can discover more about the Host who brought you to His table. Remember to thank Him for the sumptuous feast you have enjoyed from the beginning.

Continuing Education

But God made the earth by his power,
and he preserves it by his wisdom.
He has stretched out the heavens by his understanding.

Jeremiah 10:12

GETTING A MIND FULL!

O ne of the challenges for any of us is determining how we will rule out negativity. How do you keep worry from coming into your mind? Each day we're bombarded with news that delivers the tragic and the merciless things that go on at home and abroad into our psyches. If we don't worry about the world, then we worry about our jobs or our families and friends.

Howard Chandler Christy commented, "Every morning I spend fifteen minutes filling my mind full of God; and so there's no room left for worry thoughts."

Most of us need to understand that what we think shapes our actions. What we think shapes our worries or our well-being. What if we started each day thinking about God, about His goodness, His grace, His mercy, His peace, and His desire for us to live a fulfilled and abundant life? What a difference those fifteen minutes could make.

Before you go out the door as a blank slate, spend some time with God and get a mind full of Him.

CONTINUING EDUCATION

Always be full of joy in the Lord. I say it again—rejoice! Let everyone see that you are considerate in all you do.

PHILIPPIANS 4:4–5

GRACE

THERE BUT BY THE GRACE OF GOD

W hat do we really understand about grace? Each day we rise, living fully in the grace of God. Did we earn that right? Did we do anything to cause it to be possible? We receive the good things that sustain us, and we are saved from things that would harm us every single day.

Grace is what we receive from God even when we don't deserve it, and mercy is when God lovingly does not give us what we do deserve.

Perhaps the appropriate feeling to have toward grace is one of awe. "Amazing Grace" is more than a church song; it's a revelation. Today as you walk in the grace of the Lord, let your heart do a double flip and sing His praise. Give Him a way to know that you worship Him in glory and in grace for all He has done for you.

Often we see someone in far worse straits than we are and we remember the saying "There but by the grace of God go I." If you believe that and rejoice in the life you lead, share the message of grace with someone you care about and thank the One who effortlessly holds you and gives you wings.

CONTINUING EDUCATION

May the Lord be with your spirit. Grace be with you all.

2 TIMOTHY 4:22

A WORD OF GRACE

Did you ever notice what a difference it makes in your day when someone says something complimentary to you? Perhaps they tell you that you have the greatest smile they've ever seen or your ideas are incredible or your friendship means so much to them. Those are the things that much of the greeting card industry thrives on—those simple graces we extend to each other in friendship.

Words are powerful things—in a mere moment you can build someone up or totally shut them up. When you consider that God spoke the world into being, you start to see how much what you speak matters.

When you extend grace to someone with your words, put your heart into it, put your blessings into it. That is indeed what God does for you each day. Make this a day of intention about the words you speak. Extend a kind word to anyone you meet and see how it creates joy in their day—and yours!

CONTINUING EDUCATION

Let your conversation be gracious and effective so that you will have the right answer for everyone.

COLOSSIANS 4:6

Which Path to Follow

I t's not always easy to determine which path to take when you find yourself at a crossroad. How do you decide? Do you look for the easiest path? Do you look for a familiar path that may not have a high risk-and-reward ratio?

Or maybe you just decide it doesn't matter, because you don't really know where you want to end up.

Graduation means that you've accomplished one important life goal, but then the life roads open up in a lot of directions. You can find yourself like the scarecrow in the Wizard of Oz, getting your arms and legs all tangled up as you try to figure out which way to go.

If your life feels a bit like that, it's a good idea to come back and meditate on the Word of God. If you're able to trust that where you go is according to God's will and purpose for your life, then you can be sure that His grace will sustain you until it's time to chart a new course.

Embrace the paths of life and walk with courage. God will always give you a road map if you remember to include Him in your decision.

Continuing Education

"Be strong and courageous.
Do not be terrified; do not be discouraged,
for the LORD your God will be with you wherever you go."
Joshua 1:9 NIV

Does Grace Have Limits?

L ife will take you to delightful heights, and it will spiral you into shame and despair. All of it is intended to teach you one thing: God's love for you is unchanging. His grace is unlimited.

Try to remember this: "Your worst days are never so bad that you are beyond the reach of God's grace. And your best days are never so good that you are beyond the need for God's grace."

Think of that! No matter how bad things may seem, God continues to surround you with His grace and His mercy. He can still find you and reach out to you. It is you who must return the favor. You must come out of hiding and seek Him, as well.

No matter how good things are, you still need God's grace. You are never going to be so successful that you are the center of your own universe. If you find yourself there, step back, because now you may be in the *worst* position ever.

Don't take grace for granted! Give God the glory! Give God your heart and mind and soul, and He will hold you up in victory in every situation.

Continuing Education

The LORD is faithful in all he says; he is gracious in all he does.
The LORD helps the fallen and lifts up those bent beneath their loads.

PSALM 145:13–14

GOODNESS GRACIOUS!

Maybe you haven't actually stopped to think about what it means for you to live in grace. Maybe you don't literally remind yourself each day that you exist because of God's goodness! Maybe you don't, but maybe you should!

Today, challenge yourself to be very aware of grace in your life. When you walk down the street, see how your smile might extend a moment of grace to someone passing by. Share a simple hello with people you encounter who are in your space and sphere of influence no matter how temporarily.

Offer to help before anyone asks you. Be the grace that someone else needs.

You may discover a whole world of joy that you didn't realize was right in your hand and one that God alone provides for you every day.

Today, do everything you can to extend grace and mercy and love. It will surely be a blessing to those around you.

❧❧❧❧❧❧❧❧❧❧❧❧❧❧❧❧❧❧❧❧❧❧❧❧❧❧❧❧❧❧❧❧

CONTINUING EDUCATION

And God is able to make all grace abound to you,
so that in all things at all times, having all that you need,
you will abound in every good work.

2 CORINTHIANS 9:8 NIV

SAYING GRACE

S ome of you grew up saying grace before meals. It was the standard practice of your family. Some of you did not. Either way, you may have not given much thought to the practice or the reason for it. Why say grace before a meal? Is there any reason to keep doing that even when you're alone or in your own space apart from family?

If we look at the example set by Jesus, then the answer is yes. He offered a blessing, a prayer, a grace before every meal. He thanked God for providing what was needed on this very basic level of existence. He blessed the bread and it multiplied to feed thousands.

Stop for a moment before you consume one more mouthful of burger and fries. Stop and think about what is happening. Your need is being fulfilled. Your nourishment is being satisfied. Your life is being sustained.

Remember, too, that you may have worked to earn the money to buy the food, but you did not create the seed that grew the potato. Your Creator provided those things so you could enjoy today.

CONTINUING EDUCATION

And he took the five loaves and two fish,
looked up toward heaven,
and asked God's blessing on the food.

MATTHEW 14:19

The Head and the Heart

T he head grows by taking in, but the heart grows by giving out."

You're designed to grow. It is the job you're here to do. How you grow and how quickly you learn depends on this balance of head and heart. What you take and what you give are important to all that you become.

Getting an education is far more than what you take in as book knowledge and life philosophy. You may have discovered head knowledge of the Bible is a useful thing, but it will never truly help you grow until it becomes heart knowledge, as well. God speaks to the heart. It's part of the reason we say, "God is love."

As you grow in knowledge of the world and the field you choose to work in, and as you grow in relationships and friendships, look at what you're willing to give to those things. Look at how you feel when you're giving compared to how you feel when you're taking.

Grow today. Learn more, love more, and be more!

Continuing Education

But grow in the special favor and knowledge
of our Lord and Savior Jesus Christ.

2 Peter 3:18

KEEP ON WALKING

G rowth is an action. It's something you do. You can welcome it, embrace it, and let it become an intentional part of your life, or you can be surprised when it feels thrust upon you without even beckoning it. Growing happens each time we hurt, each time we fall down, and each time we must start again.

Comfort is a good thing. It's something that we aspire toward and something that makes life pleasant and rich. Comfort is inaction. It does not require anything of you. Augustine of Hippo put it this way: "If you are pleased with what you are, you have stopped already. If you say, 'It is enough,' you are lost. Keep on walking, moving forward, trying for the goal. Don't try to stop on the way, or to go back, or to deviate from it."

Growing means you keep walking. Today, walk intentionally toward those things that challenge your heart and mind and keep you aspiring to become more, give more, or believe more than you did yesterday.

CONTINUING EDUCATION

When I was a child, I talked like a child,
I thought like a child, I reasoned like a child.
When I became a man, I put childish ways behind me.

1 CORINTHIANS 13:11 NIV

BEING THE CLAY

At some time in your educational experience, you probably took an art class. When the day came to create with clay, your teacher may have suggested you work with the clay a bit to soften it and then create anything you'd like. Some people created brilliant objects, and some could only create an ashtray, no matter what they did. The experience was not so much about the object created but about the lesson of working with clay.

We are God's workmanship. He is the Potter and we are the clay. He can mold us and shape us and help us become something beautiful if we're pliable and willing to allow His handiwork to be created. His vision for us is beyond anything we can imagine. He sees us as a finished masterpiece right from the start.

When we are cold and unyielding, unwilling to allow His hand to work in our lives, we become brittle and broken. We cannot be fashioned according to His grace and divine intention. We don't realize how much He wants us to become more than an ashtray.

Are you ready to let the Master create His great work in you?

CONTINUING EDUCATION

And yet, LORD, you are our Father.
We are the clay, and you are the potter.
We are all formed by your hand.

ISAIAH 64:8

LEARNING TO FLY

The mother eagle teaches her little ones to fly by making their nest so uncomfortable that they are forced to leave it and commit themselves to the unknown world of air outside. And just so does our God to us.

HANNAH WHITALL SMITH

Graduation generally means it's time to look out for yourself. Some can hardly wait to fly. Their proverbial wings have been flapping for years, and they've already stepped beyond the bounds of the nest to know they can make it on the outside air.

Some just peek over the edge of the nest and see everything scary and think it's just not the right time to fly. They hide under Mama's wing and hope nobody brings up the topic of leaving again.

Most mamas have a hard time making it uncomfortable for their babies to leave the nest. Unlike the eagle mamas, they simply will hope you trust yourself and God enough to get out there and learn to fly. Your mama already gave you wings—the rest is up to you!

CONTINUING EDUCATION

He gives power to those who are tired and worn out; he offers strength to the weak. Even youths will become exhausted, and young men will give up. But those who wait on the LORD will find new strength. They will fly high on wings like eagles.

ISAIAH 40:29-31

HEART

GUARD YOUR HEART

Valentines and greeting cards aside, your heart needs protection. What you take to heart, deliver with heart, and share with your heart create the most important relationships in your life. As you've probably learned by now, it's not always easy to safeguard your heart.

While you were growing up, your parents or caregivers did their best to protect you physically, spiritually, and emotionally. They provided safety and love and care and kept you apart from things that might not be in your best interest.

Now that you're on your own, you may have discovered the world is not a nurturing parent. In fact, it does not have an interest in protecting you at all. How do you keep from being overwhelmed and disheartened by life?

You do it by keeping close to your heavenly parent, to the One who offers you divine protection and will be watching over you and watching out for your heart forever.

Pray when your heart is uncertain. When you aren't sure how to share your heart, pray more. Stay connected to your heart's Source.

CONTINUING EDUCATION

Above all else, guard your heart,
for it affects everything you do.

PROVERBS 4:23

Speak from the Heart

Good things like kindness and praise and affection come from the heart. We're willing to share those things with the special people in our lives. We're not always as aware that we can share those things with others we don't know as well. In other words, you can speak kindness and praise to total strangers if that is what lives in your heart.

Your heart is the guide, the headmaster of your body. It will determine how you behave and how you regard others. Whether you're in a position of serving others or being served by others, your heart's attitude will make all the difference in how you do or do not extend kindness. Speaking from a heart that overflows with kindness means you will lavish it on all those you come across.

Make it your intention today to speak from the heart to everyone. It will make a difference to each one you meet, to your own well-being. You can be sure a little cheering will go on in heaven, as well. When in doubt, let your heart go first wherever you are.

Continuing Education

"Good people have good things in their hearts,
and so they say good things."

Matthew 12:35 NCV

Set Your Heart Right

Confucius said, "To put the world in order, we must first put the nation in order; to put the nation in order, we must put the family in order; to put the family in order, we must cultivate our personal life; and to cultivate our personal life, we must first set our hearts right."

Jesus said it a little differently when He instructed us to seek God with "all your heart, all your soul, all your mind, and all your strength." So how do we set our hearts right?

We start with ourselves. We start by looking truthfully at what our hearts hope for, what attitudes are set toward others, and what thoughts we share with God. We start by saying, "Lord, create in me a clean heart."

If you begin today with a "clean heart," you create opportunity for seeking God and seeking good in all that happens to you. You can't benefit the kingdom and put nations in order, or jobs, or friends—or anything else—until you have set your heart right. See what a difference it makes!

Continuing Education

"You must love the Lord your God with all your heart, all your soul, all your mind, and all your strength."
MARK 12:30

Finding Your Heart

Y ou probably haven't lost your heart, at least not in any real sense, but as you continue on your pathway it might become more difficult to keep your heart open. You may decide that in order to protect it, you just won't share so much about yourself, or you won't care as much about other people and then you'll be safe.

Charles Spurgeon said, "Neither prayer, nor praise, nor the hearing of the Word will be profitable to those who have left their hearts behind them."

The danger then in closing your heart is that you may close it off to God, as well, making it difficult for Him to get through to you and share the joy He has planned for you. So if cynicism has crept into your spirit and you need to open a new door for your heart to feel safe in, go back to your first love. Go back to Jesus so that He can help restore your heart for the good things meant just for you.

He's waiting there for you, and His door is already open.

CONTINUING EDUCATION

"Look! Here I stand at the door and knock.
If you hear me calling and open the door,
I will come in, and we will share a meal as friends."

REVELATION 3:20

FOLLOW YOUR HEART

Whenever you have to tackle something that seems unclear or you have to make decisions about someone or something that causes you to pause for air, it may be that you're handling too much with your head and not enough with your heart. If you handle yourself with your head and others with your heart, it may lead to more hoped-for results.

The wisest of us don't have all the answers, and your friends may not have answers that are right for you, either. Those times will require discernment, prayer, and checking in with your heart to see how you really feel. Most situations become clearer with a little patience and prayer. If you follow your heart, you're sure to go the right direction.

"Follow your heart," then, is far more than a cliché. It may be the wisdom God wants you to have this very day.

CONTINUING EDUCATION

"For the LORD sees every heart and understands
and knows every plan and thought.
If you seek him, you will find him."

1 CHRONICLES 28:9

HOPE

LIVING WITH HOPE

Hope comes into our lives at an early age. We hope for a bike for our birthday or for a puppy at Christmas. Hope brings us things to dream about and imagine.

As we grow older and have more experience, we realize that hope doesn't always bring the puppy or the college scholarship. Reality doesn't always side with our dreams.

That being said, there is a certain hope that you can live with all the days of your life. It is the hope offered by our Lord and Savior, Jesus Christ. It is the hope of the ages made manifest on Christmas Day.

When your reality leaves you empty-handed, fold your hands in prayer and connect to the hope you have in Christ. Today and always, He is the Living Hope for you.

CONTINUING EDUCATION

What is faith? It is the confident assurance that what we hope for is going to happen. It is the evidence of things we cannot yet see.

HEBREWS 11:1

Living without Hope

I f you're looking at any part of your life today and believe that you don't have hope there, take another look. Shift your focus. When you suffer with an attitude of hopelessness even for a moment, you encounter frustration, loneliness, and sadness.

But is hopelessness ever really the truth? If it makes you unproductive, unable to move forward, unable to go after your dreams, then perhaps you've created a lie instead of the truth. The truth sets you free; it allows you to grow and sow and reap.

It's time to take another look. Embrace those areas of your life that you have given over to cynicism and hopelessness, and change your direction. Discover one step you can take that might open the door to the truth for you and the hope that is always available to you. Hope is the key to possibility.

Continuing Education

We also have joy with our troubles,
because we know that these troubles produce patience.
And patience produces character, and character produces hope.
And this hope will never disappoint us, because
God has poured out his love to fill our hearts.

Romans 5:3–5 ncv

HOLDING THE VISION OF HOPE

When the rains come and the storms rage, it's hard to think about the seeds that are being nourished in the ground that will grow again when the sun comes out and skies are peaceful and blue. As flowers appear, hope returns.

So it is with you. When you suffer disappointments, are let down, or are discouraged, it's hard to realize that possibility still looms around you and that God's plan for you is still taking shape even though you can't see it.

Hold on to the vision. Let hope remain, and you'll find those clouds of doubt disappearing more quickly as streams of sunlit joy brighten your path. That kind of vision can keep you moving in the direction that will create new opportunity.

When you choose to hope in God and His divine plan, all things are possible.

CONTINUING EDUCATION

We know that in everything
God works for the good of those who love him.
They are the people he called, because that was his plan.

ROMANS 8:28 NCV

INTEGRITY

Is Honesty a Lost Art?

D o you ever wonder if we've gotten so used to accepting the way of things in the world around us that we aren't even sure anymore what the honest things are? Honesty was once considered a character trait to be prized. We still refer to Lincoln as "Honest Abe," and we're even quick to remember George Washington's confession about cutting down the cherry tree.

What happened? Is it just so easy when you sit behind a computer screen to be somewhat less than honest since you're not face-to-face with whoever is on the other side? Is it that there are so many people in the world that we just assume that no one can be trusted and therefore honesty becomes some kind of thing of the past?

Will honesty remain a virtue? Give honesty a chance. Define it, deliver it, create a place where it can be seen in all the things you do. You'll feel so much better. . .honest!

CONTINUING EDUCATION

"As for you, if you walk before me in integrity of heart and uprightness. . .and do all I command and observe my decrees and laws, I will establish your royal throne over Israel forever."
1 KINGS 9:4–5 NIV

HONEST INTENTIONS

Abe Lincoln said, "I never had a policy; I have just tried to do my very best each and every day."

When you make it your goal—your honest intention—to do your best every day, you help create the opportunity for God to bless your work, your life, and your dreams. How do you do your very best each and every day? Is it even possible?

Today, challenge yourself to do your best in each thing that you have on your agenda. Do your best prayer, do your best breakfast, do your best conversation with a friend, and do your best work. At the end of the day, take note on how well you did, what you accomplished, and most of all how you felt about your effort.

Doing your best means measuring what you do with your heart and asking God to help you become more of what He intends you to be. Create your honest intentions, give them to God, and He'll bless your work and your life in everything you do.

CONTINUING EDUCATION

The good people who live honest lives will be a blessing to their children.

PROVERBS 20:7 NCV

SETTING THE BAR FOR YOURSELF

W hen you watch a high jumper, you know that his goal is to have the strength, the energy, and the power to jump high enough to get above the bar and safely over to the mat on the other side without hitting the bar or making it fall. When the jumper does well, the bar is set higher and a new opportunity is put before him.

How high have you set the bar of integrity for yourself? Do you work hard to have the real power it takes to achieve your goals? Do you try to catch yourself when the tiny deceptions creep into your thinking and make it harder and harder to reach the goal?

When you operate as a person of integrity, you must seek that in every area of your life. You must set the bar high for your personal life, your work life, and your life with God.

As you look at life today, see if you can spot any places where you've allowed something less than your goal to be okay. If so, aim a little higher. You'll be glad you did.

❈ ❈

CONTINUING EDUCATION

"What good is it for a man to gain the whole world, yet forfeit his soul?"

MARK 8:36 NIV

Being Honest with Yourself

Sometimes you have to take a chance and risk it all! This risk isn't about investing your money or trying a new hairstyle; it's about being honest with yourself. It's standing in front of the mirror and talking to the person you see there and clearing the air.

Does that mean you have to stand there and belittle yourself out of some false sense of modesty? No, it means you have to be fair and square about the things you tell yourself. It means stepping up to the plate and owning the way you think, act, dress, and maneuver through life.

It shouldn't be difficult, but it can be. If you've never tried to understand your own truth before, then how can anyone else really know you and know what you're about? So take three deep breaths, go to the mirror, and start a dialogue. The person looking back at you is anxious to get personally acquainted.

This encounter could make the whole rest of your life more authentic. It's time to be honest with yourself!

Continuing Education

May you receive more and more of God's mercy, peace, and love.

Jude 2

HONEST TO GOD

W hen some people want to make a point or make it clear that they are really being sincere, they'll say something like, "Honest to God, it's true!" It's an interesting phrase, because it usually means the person is saying something that requires a little faith to be believed, so they bring in God's name to give their point more validity.

The point for you today is that besides learning to be honest with yourself, it's important for you to learn to be honest with God. Whatever you do is already known to Him, so it seems odd that we would even try to hide behind the bushes and not come out when He calls, thinking somehow He won't see us. The truth is, He always sees us, and the good news is, He always sees us in the very best light.

God knows what we are capable of becoming, and His wisdom and strength are given to us to help us become the masterpieces He had in mind. If we try to shrink back from His presence, go out there on our own, and work our way around what we believe He might be asking us to do, we'll find ourselves sitting like Jonah in the belly of a whale. Your whale may not be a literal one, but you may find yourself in a fishy situation.

Delight in what God has planned for your life and step out, reach out, and embrace His direction. It will make a difference!

CONTINUING EDUCATION

The godly walk with integrity.

PROVERBS 20:7

KINDNESS

Do It with a Smile!

H ave you ever noticed how different your day is when you greet it with a smile and a positive attitude? It's almost bizarre how many complete strangers will actually speak to you or give you a nod or smile simply because your face is lit up and welcomes them to say hello.

On the contrary, those who have abandoned smiling for the more gloomy aspect will seldom notice or find that others exist, much less show they care about them at all.

If a smile is the universal language of kindness, you need to become adept at speaking it every chance you get. After all, you're a vessel for the Spirit of the Living God, and if that doesn't make you smile, it's hard to imagine what can.

Go out today and be a light, simply by being willing to share a joyful face.

CONTINUING EDUCATION

A cheerful look brings joy to the heart.

PROVERBS 15:30

Taking Kindness on the Journey

William Penn wisely said, "If there is any kindness I can show, or any good thing I can do to any fellow being, let me do it now, and not deter or neglect it, as I shall not pass this way again."

Your life journey will take you on paths you never dreamed you'd travel.

You will meet people on your way who will never cross your path again. How will you leave them? Will they remember a perfect stranger who was kind enough to say hello or lend a hand or donate to a cause? Will they reflect on the moment you shared with them as a bright spot?

Kindness does that. Kindness opens doors to wordless conversations and embraces weak souls and downhearted spirits. Kindness is always an option. Don't get tired of being kind.

Continuing Education

Don't get tired of helping others.
You will be rewarded when the time is right, if you don't give up.
We should help people whenever we can,
especially if they are followers of the Lord.

GALATIANS 6:9–10 CEV

As Kind as Mother Teresa

Few people have the kindness of heart that was often attributed to the late Mother Teresa. She devoted her life to helping others and was an amazing example of what it means to be selfless. The following is a quote from her that is worth reading at least once a day.

"Spread love everywhere you go; first of all in your own house. Let no one ever come to you without leaving better and happier. Be the living expression of God's kindness; kindness in your face, kindness in your eyes, kindness in your smile, kindness in your warm greeting."

What would it be like if more of us were the "living expression of God's kindness"? The thought is overwhelming and paints a picture of utter beauty. We can't really do anything about how others treat the world or treat us, but we can do something about how we treat them. Make this your day to be a living expression of God's kindness.

CONTINUING EDUCATION

Dear children, let us stop just saying we love each other;
let us really show it by our actions.
It is by our actions that we know we are living in the truth,
so we will be confident when we stand before the Lord.

1 JOHN 3:18–19

THE BUSINESS OF KINDNESS

We don't often think of high-powered business executives as being the kindest people we know. Some are, some aren't. The point is that you never have to leave your willingness to be kind at the door when you go to work or when you go to class or when you go anywhere at all.

As the character of Scrooge says in Dickens's *Christmas Carol*, "Mankind is my business." Mankind is always our business. We're more apt to say "humankind" today, but we understand that what we're after is the Christlike care and feeding of those around us.

Samuel Johnson once said, "Getting money is not all a man's business: To cultivate kindness is a valuable part of the business of life."

Cultivate kindness wherever you are, and see if you discover neighbors you never knew you had.

CONTINUING EDUCATION

All of you should be of one mind,
full of sympathy toward each other,
loving one another with tender hearts and humble minds.

1 PETER 3:8

BEYOND THE RANDOM ACTS

A few years ago a book came out called *Random Acts of Kindness*, and the success of it was a reminder of how much we all need to be caught in the act. We sometimes forget there are a lot of us here on this spinning ball, and we need to help each other a whole lot more than we do.

Now that you're out on your own, it's time to see what you can do to help others. When you commit an act of kindness or charity, it makes your view of the world change. For one thing, it helps you step outside of yourself long enough to be compassionate and giving.

Rude, crude, and indifferent have all had a field day out there, and it's going to take some people with an intention toward change to make things better. Be part of the change: Join the kindness revolution.

CONTINUING EDUCATION

Be kind to each other, tenderhearted, forgiving one another, just as God through Christ has forgiven you.

EPHESIANS 4:32

The Name of Kindness

D o you ever feel invisible? Do you wonder if anyone knows you're actually there? Of course, the people in your family know you, but you might be astonished to realize that most people, maybe even your neighbors, won't take time to know you or even to acknowledge you.

Consider an experiment.

Make it your business to get to know the names of people in your neighborhood. Find out the name of the person who delivers your mail or the person who leaves your newspaper. Make it a habit to learn people's names when they perform a service for you. Your grocer, your dry cleaner, and the person who picks up the trash are all real people.

If you practice getting to know people's names, you'll discover a valuable life lesson. Few people ever want to feel invisible, and most would welcome the idea that someone connected with them on a very real and personal level.

Consider it a great act of kindness to get to know your neighbor. Consider it a way to love one another.

❀❀❀❀❀❀❀❀❀❀❀❀❀❀❀❀❀❀❀❀❀❀❀❀❀❀❀❀❀❀❀❀❀❀❀❀❀❀

Continuing Education

"Love your neighbor as yourself."

Matthew 19:19 NIV

The Strength of Kindness

We tend to see power as something that is held by people who are of great wealth, great intelligence, or great position in the world. We think of kings and presidents and captains of industry. But are those the only seats of power, or do they simply appear powerful?

One Jewish tradition says, "There are ten strong things. Iron is strong, but fire melts it. Fire is strong, but water quenches it. Water is strong, but the clouds evaporate it. Clouds are strong, but wind drives them away. Man is strong, but fears cast him down. Fear is strong, but sleep overcomes it. Sleep is strong, yet death is stronger. But loving-kindness survives death."

Perhaps power then is a perception. Perhaps the most powerful person you know is the neighbor who welcomes friends and strangers alike to her table and offers a smile and lends a hand to those in need. Her power is not manmade. Her power comes from the living spirit of kindness Himself.

Let this be the beginning of your inner power. The more you give away, the more you have. Funny, it's a lot like love then.

Continuing Education

Do not withhold good from those who deserve it when it's in your power to help them. If you can help your neighbor now, don't say, "Come back tomorrow, and then I'll help you."

Proverbs 3:27–28

LEARNING

The Age of Reason

Since you've graduated, the question arises as to your intentions about learning. Will you now stop learning? Will you determine that you've gotten all you need in the school of life and from here on out you're ready to just walk into the sunset?

Of course, you know the answer. It's about realizing, as Henry Ford said, that "anyone who stops learning is old, whether at twenty or eighty." You never want to stop learning. Formal learning is only the tip of the iceberg. Everything else is still hidden beneath the surface and awaits your discovery. That's where the real learning begins. That's where you'll get a glimpse of how much there is yet to know.

It's reasonable to take a break from formal learning. It's impossible to get a break from life learning. You'll be a student all your life even if you have a Ph.D. If you get that degree in theology, it will just be the beginning of learning what God has in store for you. You've reached the age of reason. This is the age when you discover that not everything has a reason, but everything gives you a reason to learn something new.

Keep studying!

Continuing Education

Let the wise listen and add to their learning,
and let the discerning get guidance.

Proverbs 1:5 niv

GETTING IN THE GAME

When it comes to learning, you have two basic choices. You can sit along the sidelines of life and observe, learn all the rules, review the plays, and stay pretty much on the outside. In fact, you don't have to get personally involved in your own life if you don't want to.

The other choice is to get in the game. That means you may not catch the ball very often, and you may fall in the mud. You may get knocked down and have to get up and try again. You may get along well with your team, or you may end up battling it out on the playing field. You've got the choice.

It looks like the sidelines might be the better choice. You're not as apt to get beat up out there, and you can stay safe and you'll know how to predict most things before they happen, and in general, you'll be okay. You may also be bored to tears, but that's another issue.

Be encouraged today to get into the game. Play hard. Do your best and let the Coach know that you're willing to be used in any position He thinks you'd be good at. Remember, He's the only One who knows all the players.

Get out there and score!

CONTINUING EDUCATION

I discipline my body like an athlete, training it to do what it should.

1 CORINTHIANS 9:27

LIFE

Is It All about You?

O f course you've never really thought it was "all about you," but there are people in the world who do think they might be the center of the known universe, and that's worth musing about.

On one hand, it's not all about you, but on another hand, perhaps it is. After all, Jesus died for you personally, and if you had been the only one He came to save, He would have done so. Therefore, it really is all about you!

How your life comes together is all about you. It's all about the choices you make, the friends you keep, and the willingness of your heart to pay attention, to grow, and to become more.

Just for a little while today, let it be all about you. Look at yourself and check in to see where you stand in terms of attitude, perceptions, and love. Make it a positive thing to be all about you so that there's a lot of you to share in all the right ways with everyone else. Then you can shift back to making it all about *them*.

Continuing Education

"God loved the world so much that he gave his one and only Son so that whoever believes in him may not be lost, but have eternal life."

John 3:16 ncv

Using Your Talents

E rma Bombeck said, "When I stand before God at the end of my life, I would hope that I would not have a single bit of talent left and could say, 'I used everything You gave me.'"

Most of us have talents and special gifts that we recognize as being ours alone and ones God gave us. You can usually pick out the talents that your friends have, and they know yours.

If you don't yet know what your gifts are, start to explore those things that you have a passion for, or the things that you've thought about since you were a kid but haven't really tried. You may have talents you're not even aware of yet that are just begging for attention.

This is the right time in your life to find out what makes you a unique and beautiful light in the world. Have fun with it, and let your light shine.

Continuing Education

There are different kinds of spiritual gifts,
but they all come from the same Spirit.
There are different ways to serve the same Lord,
and we can each do different things.
Yet the same God works in all of us
and helps us in everything we do.

1 Corinthians 12:4–6 CEV

What Is Quiet Desperation?

Henry David Thoreau said, "The mass of men lead lives of quiet desperation."

How can you lead a life that is more like the one Jesus promised in John 10:10 (CEV) when He said, "I came so that everyone would have life, and have it in its fullest"?

What makes the difference between a life of quiet desperation and one that is lived to the fullest? The difference is often one of attitude.

If you have an attitude of joy and thanksgiving in all circumstances, regardless of what appears to be around you, your life is enriched. If you have an attitude of giving regardless of what you have to gain, you're more likely to experience fullness.

Quiet desperation is about worry; it's about closing the door on possibility; it's about closing your heart and mind to the abundance promised you by a powerful and loving Father.

You are the child of a King who wants to lavish all good things on you. If you find yourself living in quiet desperation, you might not be sitting close enough to His throne.

Continuing Education

*Every good and perfect gift comes down from
the Father who created all the lights in the heavens.*

James 1:17 CEV

INTENTIONS AND ACTIONS

E ach day we rise up with plans and intentions for the things we hope to accomplish that day. We may not always write them on a list, but we have a fair idea of what we need to get done. If we look at the list and it seems overwhelming, we may be tempted to postpone or even eliminate some of the items there. Which ones?

Start with an action. Action is always needed to get the ball rolling and motivate your steps. The action that is most important, especially when you're extremely busy, is to stop—and pray.

The first action item on your daily list is prayer. It is the one thing that will help you line up all your activities with the will of God for you. It's the opportunity to invite God into your space and create room in your heart and mind to receive the blessings He has already prepared for you.

Make prayer your intention, make prayer your action, and all your plans will succeed. You won't be spinning in circles; you'll be walking on the right path.

CONTINUING EDUCATION

It seems to be a fact of life that when I want to do what is right,
I inevitably do what is wrong.

ROMANS 7:21

LIFE OF FAITH

As believers, we strive to walk in faith and serve God. We want to do our best and deliver on the promises that we make to Him. It sounds like a plan, but it isn't always an easy plan to fulfill. How then do we get to really live a life of faith?

St. Augustine offered a glimpse into what we can do when he shared this thought: "Order your soul; reduce your wants; live in charity, associate in Christian community; obey the laws, trust in Providence."

Let's look at these one at a time:

- Order your soul—Give priority to the matters of your faith, your beliefs, and your times of prayer and meditation.
- Reduce your wants—Be content with what you have.
- Live in charity—Consider others above yourself.
- Associate in Christian community—Go to Bible study, attend church, and help others any way you can; love your neighbor.
- Obey the laws—We are subject to the authorities of others, who, in turn, are subject to the authority of God.
- Trust in Providence—Trust that God sees you, knows you, and created you with great joy and purpose.

Practice these things, and you will indeed be living a life of faith.

✿✿✿✿✿✿✿✿✿✿✿✿✿✿✿✿✿✿✿✿✿✿✿✿✿✿✿✿

CONTINUING EDUCATION

Teach us to use wisely all the time we have.

PSALM 90:12 CEV

WINNERS AND LOSERS

We live in a world of constant competition and have a tendency to measure things by wins and losses. We even measure our self-worth by whether we feel we were successful at something we did or whether we failed. Let's look at the framework of winning and losing and see what the standards really are.

- Winners choose to be part of the answer; losers choose to add to the problem.
- Winners choose to find solutions; losers choose to find excuses.
- Winners choose to "get it done"; losers choose to leave the job to someone else.
- Winners choose to find the "yes"; losers choose to see the "no."
- Winners choose to find the possible even when it's difficult; losers tend to find the difficult, even when it's possible.
- Winners choose to walk with God; losers choose to walk around God.

Life offers continual opportunities for winning and losing. How you settle the score depends on the choices you make. Walk with God, and come out a winner!

CONTINUING EDUCATION

"If you love your life, you will lose it.
If you give it up in this world, you will be given eternal life."

JOHN 12:25 CEV

READ THE MANUAL

D o you ever wish your life had some kind of manual you could refer to when things get sticky or you simply don't know which direction to go or how to handle what's coming next?

Your manual may not have come with your name specifically written in the upper left corner, but you came into the world with a fully developed plan and a guidebook, nonetheless. It's called the Bible. By now, you have either fully embraced or somewhat ignored the manual, but it's waiting for you to dust off the pages and look for the treasures meant just for you.

When we get something new—let's say a new computer— and we've had one before, we're tempted to not read the enclosed manual because we think we already know all about it. To our surprise, when something happens that we don't understand, we discover some new things have been programmed into this model that we needed to learn about.

Think of yourself as God's model, already programmed, but still in need of refining and defining the important steps that make you operate fully and joyfully. There may still be things to learn. Check around; you'll find a manual somewhere.

CONTINUING EDUCATION

"For the Spirit of God has made me,
and the breath of the Almighty gives me life."
JOB 33:4

THE MEANING OF LIFE

Graduation is a good time to look at the meaning of life. It's good to understand our purpose and why we were born and what God truly wants from us. It's good to know what the earth school is about and how we can graduate with honors.

The Bible offers help through the writings of King Solomon in Ecclesiastes. King Solomon was one of the wisest and best-known rulers of his time. He had great wealth and power and unusual knowledge. Yet even he reflected on the meaning of life and came, in part, to this conclusion:

"The best thing we can do is to enjoy eating, drinking, and working. I believe these are God's gifts to us, and no one enjoys eating and living more than I do. If we please God, he will make us wise, understanding, and happy. But if we sin, God will make us struggle for a living, then he will give all we own to someone who pleases him" (Ecclesiastes 2:24–26 CEV).

Solomon reminds us to enjoy what we have. Enjoy living today while you're making breakfast, sharing moments with friends, or working on a project. God will bless your efforts, and your life will be meaningful.

CONTINUING EDUCATION

Everything that happens has happened before, and all that will be has already been— God does everything over and over again.

ECCLESIASTES 3:15 CEV

GETTING WHAT YOU WANT

No doubt when you graduated from high school or college, your first plan was to go out into the world and start creating the path that would lead to getting what you want. Whether you want more education, a good job, a new relationship, or an opportunity to live somewhere totally new, you're ready to get there. That's all good!

As a Christian, you know God honors the desires of your heart, hears your prayers, and guides your steps. He provides what you need in order to get what you want. However, have you ever looked back at things you wanted that you didn't get and heaved a sigh of relief? Sometimes not getting what we want is the best gift God can give us.

As you go after what you want, make sure you consider all the angles you can. Make sure you start with prayer, go to the Guidebook for specific help, and wait on the Lord. If you get there ahead of Him, you may not find the answers you were expecting. If you walk beside Him, you may see things you never saw before. Getting what you want just might take on a whole new meaning.

CONTINUING EDUCATION

It's better to enjoy what we have
than to always want something else,
because that makes no more sense than chasing the wind.

ECCLESIASTES 6:9 CEV

Things Worth Remembering

The longer you live, the more there is for you to remember. Guidelines for the work ahead of you may prove helpful. The following is a list of things to remember, points to ponder, and ideas to incubate.

- Your character is worth protecting.
- Your time is always valuable.
- Your success takes great perseverance.
- Your talent can always be improved.
- Your friends sustain you.
- Your work should bring great pleasure.
- Your kindness brings power.
- Your wisdom brings peace.
- Your Father in heaven knows your name.

You can continue the list with things you know that are worth remembering. Create your own personal one, filling in the word *your* with your name, and see what focus it brings to you. Laugh, dance, and live as a light in the hearts of those around you.

Continuing Education

"The eye is the lamp of the body. If your eyes are good, your whole body will be full of light."

Matthew 6:22 niv

IN THE LIGHT OF GOD'S GOODNESS

Y ou have a choice in the way you see your life. You can
either see the unfulfilled and drab aspects of your days,
the lonely and tired grayness of your nights, or you can set your
vision toward the light and let a whole new world emerge.

Albert Schweitzer put it this way: "Your life is something
opaque, not transparent, as long as you look at it in an ordinary
human way. But if you hold it up against the light of God's
goodness, it shines and turns transparent, radiant and bright.
And then you ask yourself in amazement: 'Is this really my
own life I see before me?' "

As you look at your life today, try holding it up against
the "light of God's goodness" and see what you discover. See
if you radiate in the joy of knowing you are in His care and
that you are loved just as you are. You are God's light in the
world, and you need to shine for Him in every way possible.
See yourself in the best possible light.

CONTINUING EDUCATION

*The one who is the true light, who gives light to everyone,
was going to come into the world.*

JOHN 1:9

Spreading Light

A very well-known quote by Edith Wharton says, "There are two ways of spreading light; to be the candle or the mirror that reflects it." Today we have no end of light sources, so you could be the floodlight, the solar panel, or perhaps some form of incandescence, but in one form or another, you have the opportunity to be the light. If, indeed, you don't feel you can be the light, then you must at least reflect the light for others.

In your walk of faith, you will be one or the other. You may not be an evangelist or a door-to-door Bible salesman, but you might still be someone who shares the light every way possible. You shine each time you give from your heart, helping another in distress, sharing a smile with an elderly person, or simply being kind to those around you. You shine each time you share your faith and your love for God. You are the light.

Some days you may not want to turn your light on. At those times, all you want to do is acknowledge the light in others, find joy in the light someone else gives you, or rest in the spirit of grace. Either way, you end up a part of the light and adding a bit more warmth to the darkness.

Continuing Education

Many people say, "Who will show us better times?"
Let the smile of your face shine on us, LORD.

PSALM 4:6

Free and Light

The Bible says that "the light shines in the darkness" (John 1:5 NIV). In a literal sense, we understand we do not see the stars in the sky until the darkness appears. The stars are there all day as well, but we don't realize their presence.

Light fills every space it can without seeking anything in return. It simply does what it is designed to do. It shines.

We are like that, too. We are designed to fill in the dark spaces and let our light shine. We don't have to ask if we can do it. We don't have to wait until we're a certain age to flip the switch; we just have to be what we are—light in the world. We have to move about in the darkness and let the truth of who we are escape into every corner of the globe.

Who are we? We're the children of God, who carry His light into the darkness. We're His stars at night and His sunshine during the day. We're the reason He came in person to redeem us. As redeemed children, we're ready to shine all the time. Isn't it time for a chorus of "This Little Light of Mine"?

❖❖❖❖❖❖❖❖❖❖❖❖❖❖❖❖❖❖❖❖❖❖❖❖❖❖❖❖❖❖❖❖❖❖❖❖❖

Continuing Education

"You are like light for the whole world. . . .
Make your light shine, so that others will see the good
that you do and will praise your Father in heaven."
MATTHEW 5:14, 16 CEV

LIGHT IN THE SOUL

If there is light in the soul,
There will be beauty in the person.
If there is beauty in the person,
There will be harmony in the house.
If there is harmony in the house,
There will be order in the nation.
If there is order in the nation,
There will be peace in the world.

CHINESE PROVERB

This beautiful proverb reminds us of the importance of having light in your heart and soul. How do you get that light? You get that light from tapping into the ultimate Source, the Creator God, who sees you and offers you His light through His Son, Jesus.

The Light of the World came so that you could truly reflect Him to others. His light makes you beautiful and brings harmony to your home and peace to those around you.

Today, be the light. Illuminate the path of everyone you meet.

CONTINUING EDUCATION

For you are all children of the light and of the day;
we don't belong to darkness and night.

1 THESSALONIANS 5:5

MAKING THE "LIGHT" CHOICE

H ave you noticed all the Hummers on the road these days? You know, those vehicles that look like they came right from the battlefield of life, designed with tons of steel to protect the passenger from—well, who knows what? It's interesting that we would choose to take something with a warlike attitude and try to give it a domestic spin.

Those of us who live in God's light have more protection than a Hummer could ever offer. We walk in the armor of light. It's designed in a style that fits us all. The price for it was paid long ago, and the opportunity to go into battle with it exists indefinitely.

When we made the Light choice, we said, "Okay, give me all you've got, World, because I can take it. I'm fully equipped to meet you head-on. I'm protected by the Light of the World."

When you made the Light choice, that was a humdinger! Go out and let the world see you coming!

CONTINUING EDUCATION

Nothing exists that he didn't make. Life itself was in him, and this life gives light to everyone.

JOHN 1:3–4

LOVE

LEARNING TO LOVE

D oes it seem odd to consider that love might just be a subject to be taught, a course to be taken, a thing to be studied well before you enter into it? Certainly there's plenty of evidence to suggest that people engaged in romantic love aren't especially good at keeping it going or fanning its flames.

We've been taught that God is love, and though we accept that someplace in our brains, we may not actually understand what it means in truth. So how do we engage in, create, and learn more about what love really is? We're always bandying the word around as though we know something about it. We say we "love" chocolate, or we "love" our cat, or we "love" someone, but maybe we need further education.

This week, think about what you know about love—romantic love, love for your neighbor, love for God, love for family. Are you acquainted enough with love to be its ambassador? Do you need to study a bit more? The world is your classroom, and it offers courses at all levels from remedial to graduate school. Your love diploma awaits.

CONTINUING EDUCATION

You must teach people to have genuine love, as well as a good conscience and true faith.

1 TIMOTHY 1:5 CEV

About That "Love Your Neighbor" Thing

O ne of the wonderful things about the Bible is that many of the commands seem so incredibly simple and yet remain mysterious. "Love your neighbor" is one of those. We may think we know what that means and that we do it because we don't bully our neighbor, or we help people when we have time, or we give to a charity, but is that really the message?

What makes it so easy or hard to "love your neighbor"? Part of the answer is that whether we realize it or not, we try to define which neighbors we're going to love. We tend to choose to "love" the neighbors who think a lot like we do, go to our church, or work in the same place. It's good and right to love them. The question is, what about all the rest of the neighbors?

Expand your list of "neighbors." Today, make it a conscious choice to show love to someone you may not have even noticed before. It'll give you some new insight, and it'll be a downright neighborly thing to do!

❈❈❈❈❈❈❈❈❈❈❈❈❈❈❈❈❈❈❈❈❈❈❈❈❈❈❈❈❈❈❈

Continuing Education

"Love your neighbor as yourself."

Mark 12:31 niv

What Does It Mean to Love Yourself?

The gospel says to "love your neighbor as yourself." Well, what if you were pretty happy with yourself yesterday and treated everyone nicely, and as far as you could tell, you understand this command?

But then today you're not so happy with yourself, and so you grouse at those around you and spill your insecurities out on the ones who care about you the most, and before you know it, the day is really miserable.

It appears that it's not so easy to love your neighbor when you simply don't love yourself. When you're the chief judge and jury and critic for everything you do, what happens to how you treat everyone else? It seems reasonable that your perceptions about the world have a lot to do with your perceptions about yourself.

Give yourself a break today. See if you can stop being a critic, stop making yourself out to be the bad guy, and like yourself in all the real, positive, and God-given ways you were meant to be liked and loved. See how that attitude affects your ability to love your neighbor. Take it as a challenge if you must.

Continuing Education

Be devoted to one another in brotherly love.
Honor one another above yourselves.

Romans 12:10 NIV

LOVE IS A VERB

L ove always requires action. In fact, love demands action.
Love isn't content to be passive and sit on the sidelines
while other things push and shove their way ahead of it. Love
says, "Stand up and be noticed. Shout out that I'm here.
Make me a priority."

If it doesn't, then it may not really be love. Think of the
top three people you've ever loved. Maybe you listed a parent
or a friend or a sibling or God. Didn't every one of them
demand your action, your attention, your participation?

Today, when you think about someone you love, or when
you think about your love for God, think about what action
you need to take to show how real your love is. What can you
do in even a small way to let the object of your affection
know you are really in love? Did you figure it out? Now, go
and do it.

CONTINUING EDUCATION

May the Lord make your love for each other
and for everyone else grow by leaps and bounds.

1 THESSALONIANS 3:12 CEV

GETTING LOVE TO ADD UP

I n a romantic sense, we like to think that one plus one equals two—together, becoming one. Odd math, but emotionally we get it. In that same addition, if we partner with someone and add God's love to the mix, we have a threefold cord. Now we are stronger and less apt to break.

So why doesn't love add up more often? Why isn't love the answer? We see LOVE IS THE ANSWER embroidered on pillow covers, but in truth, it seems fragile and elusive.

Maybe love adds up somewhat better if you start this way: Focus on your first love, God. Then reflect on His love for you and then share all that love with each one you meet. Before you know it, love is adding up again. Everywhere you go, you can see love, share love, be love, and help love to grow.

If love does not seem to be growing in your life, check to see how much of it you're giving away. In the mathematics of love, the more you give away, the more you have left. Need a calculator?

CONTINUING EDUCATION

Love is more important than anything else.
It is what ties everything completely together.

COLOSSIANS 3:14 CEV

Love and the Body of Christ

The good news is we're all different from each other. The bad news is we're all different from each other. The fact that we aren't clones means we have to learn about the things that make each one of us unique and the things that also make each of us the same.

If we take it as a given that God loves each one of us and created each of us for a purpose, then we pretty much have the idea of what makes us more alike than different. If we take that same premise and understand that we each have significant gifts that we're intended to use, then we can appreciate our differences.

As the body of Christ in some literal sense, as His heart and mind and spirit here on earth, we have to each love as He loves us and share the gifts we've been given.

Your job is to grow in His love for you and in the gifts you've been given.

Continuing Education

Each one of you is part of the body of Christ,
and you were chosen to live together in peace.

Colossians 3:15 CEV

LOVE AND JUDGMENT

Mother Teresa said, "If you judge people, you have no time to love them."

We're always making judgments. Having good judgment is an important aspect of making wise choices. Having good judgment and being a judge are two different things.

Most of us don't really recognize how very judgmental we are. If we stop to think about it, we might see we play the judgment card fairly often. It may be in little ways, like noticing someone isn't dressed very well or needs to comb their hair, or it may be in much bigger ways where we decide that we don't like someone just because they have a different skin color or mannerism. We might even make instant assumptions. We'd probably never recognize the carpenter as the King.

Judging isn't really our domain. Loving is. God commands that we love one another. He didn't say, "Judge one another." Give yourself more time to love others today.

CONTINUING EDUCATION

*Most important of all,
continue to show deep love for each other,
for love covers a multitude of sins.*

1 PETER 4:8

LOVE AND COMPASSION

One of the blessings we have in receiving God's love is that we also receive His compassion. That means He is continually giving us His grace, mercy, and understanding. It means He knows us so well that He wants to offer us comfort and sympathy and kindness.

He intends for us to share His love with others. He is our example of what compassion looks like. Any day of the week, we realize how grateful we are for the compassion our Creator has toward us. How can we share that same grace and mercy with others?

Let's practice being God's people of compassion. Let's listen with sympathy to one another and embrace each other's needs. Let's be kinder than we have ever been before and stretch ourselves to offer empathy and love in situations that may be unfamiliar ground.

There's no place you can go to be outside of God's compassion for you. Let it be said that anywhere you go you offer that same gift of compassion to others.

CONTINUING EDUCATION

God loves you and has chosen you as his own special people.
So be gentle, kind, humble, meek, and patient.
Put up with each other, and forgive anyone who does you wrong,
just as Christ has forgiven you.

COLOSSIANS 3:12–13 CEV

If You Have a Little Love

W hat if you see yourself as being a person who only has a little love to give away? Let's say you have a cup of love to give your neighbor. You walk to your neighbor's house and knock on the door. You imagine that you'll offer your little cup of love and be done with your "duty" for the day.

When your neighbor answers and sees you standing there with your cup, a smile lights their face. They stand before you with a small cup as well and now there are two of you each holding your simple cup of love.

You extend your hand and give a blessing for the day and offer to help your neighbor if any need exists and hand over your cup. To your surprise, your neighbor is holding a much larger cup now, but so are you. This exchange goes back and forth until both of you are illuminated with love, and as you walk away, you realize how much you've received from the little you expected to give.

Have you ever noticed that when you mean to give only a little, you often walk away with a lot? If you haven't, take your little cup of love over to your neighbor and see what happens.

Continuing Education

Let love be your highest goal,
but also desire the special abilities the Spirit gives.

1 Corinthians 14:1

The Language of Love

The Bible talks about speaking "in any language in heaven or on earth" as though that would be a marvelous thing. In the next breath, it says that even though it would be remarkable to be able to do that, it wouldn't have any meaning if it was done without love. It would be a "meaningless noise," like a "clanging cymbal."

Does it ever seem to you that we're pretty good at making noises about love? We have the outward appearance of love, or we say the right words that should mean love, or we might even act in a way that seems like love, but sometimes those things don't add up to anything but noise. We're empty vessels with nothing to give.

What is your language of love? How do you express your heart and mind and share with truth and light the love you feel? Listen carefully today to your own love language. Are you a clanging cymbal of noise or a symphony of love?

Continuing Education

If I could speak in any language in heaven or on earth but didn't love others, I would only be making meaningless noise like a loud gong or a clanging cymbal.

1 Corinthians 13:1

NATURE

THE GOSPEL OF TREES AND FLOWERS

When you've had enough of pursuing and planning and working and doing, it's often a good idea to take yourself on a walk with God. When you do that, you may see things that you miss in the hustle and bustle of your routine.

Martin Luther said, "God writes the gospel not in the Bible alone, but on trees and flowers and clouds and stars."

How many sermons have you missed by not taking the pathless woods or the peaceful moments by the riverside? God often can speak louder when you're quieter and more at rest. He always has good news to share with you, so why not grab a picnic basket and head out for some good old-fashioned gospel moments? God is already there.

CONTINUING EDUCATION

Did you ever tell the sun to rise? And did it obey?
Did it take hold of the earth and shake out
the wicked like dust from a rug?
Early dawn outlines the hills like stitches
on clothing or sketches on clay.

JOB 38:12–14 CEV

Take a Walk on the Wild Side

O kay, this is about taking a walk outside, in the wild— that is, in nature. You need a break today. You need to be refreshed and enriched and made whole, and God has designed this planet to give you opportunities for that to happen. You just need to take advantage of them.

John Muir wrote, "Climb the mountains and get their good tidings. Nature's peace will flow into you as sunshine flows into trees. The winds will blow their own freshness into you, and the storms their energy, while cares will drop off like autumn leaves."

If it's time for you to get away from it all for a little while, see what the winds and the trees and the birds have to teach you. You might be surprised at their wisdom. They were all created just for you.

Continuing Education

The heavens declare the glory of God;
the skies proclaim the work of his hands.

Psalm 19:1 niv

PATIENCE

ARE YOU WILLING TO WAIT?

You may sometimes find yourself in a battle between what you want and what it appears God wants for you. When you do, you have to make a choice. The easy one is to do what you want. Or is it?

Making decisions is part of living, and many of your choices don't carry enough consequence to matter on an eternal level. But what happens when you recognize that you are not getting something you want and are starting to get the idea that maybe it's God who does not want that particular thing for you? Then what? Are you willing to be patient and try to understand God more clearly?

Hebrews 10:36 says, "Patient endurance is what you need now, so you will continue to do God's will. Then you will receive all that he has promised."

"Patient endurance" is easier to write and speak about than to sit and wait for. Patience by itself is never easy, but "patient endurance" seems to imply some difficulty in the waiting. Your will or God's will? Isn't that often the question? What's your answer?

CONTINUING EDUCATION

The LORD is wonderfully good to those who wait for him and seek him. So it is good to wait quietly for salvation from the LORD. And it is good for the young to submit to the yoke of his discipline.

LAMENTATIONS 3:25–27

THE TROUBLE WITH PATIENCE

D id you ever have one of those days when it seems like the whole world is out of sync with you? You sleep late so your day is already backed up. You reach for the paper and see it out near the street and it's pouring down rain. You finally get on your way, and the traffic lights are out in your neighborhood, and you know your boss is steaming already because you aren't there. . . .

Should you just call it a day and go back home and crawl in bed? Well, that can seem like the right answer, but maybe this kind of day needs another approach. Maybe the trouble with patience is that we assume it means everything is hard, so we have to endure it.

Could it be that the patience we need isn't with the outside world at all? Could it be that from the first alarm that got us up late we needed a course correction for our attitude? What if we had stopped the world, gotten on our knees, and asked God to take over from here because we already blew it from anything we could tell. The world may have looked different from that moment on. Try it and see.

CONTINUING EDUCATION

Whatever is good and perfect comes to us
from God above, who created all heaven's lights.
Unlike them, he never changes or casts shifting shadows.

JAMES 1:17

CLOTHE YOURSELF IN PATIENCE

L eonardo da Vinci was one of the great artists, philo-
sophers, and scientists of his day. He said, "Patience
serves as a protection against wrongs as clothes do against
cold. For if you put on more clothes as the cold increases,
it will have no power to hurt you. So in like manner, you must
grow in patience when you meet with great wrongs, and they
will be powerless to vex your mind."

In other words, if you practice clothing yourself with
patience when those little life irritations start to get to you,
you'll be much more equipped when real troubles come along
to handle them in a manner that does not make you crazy.

Practice patience! Prepare yourself to handle things
calmly when they are simple and not in your control—like
waiting in line at the grocery store or discovering your cable
TV is out. You may find patience to be one of the best outfits
you ever wear.

CONTINUING EDUCATION

*Clothe yourselves with tenderhearted mercy,
kindness, humility, gentleness, and patience.
You must make allowance for each other's faults
and forgive the person who offends you.*

COLOSSIANS 3:12-13

BEING A BIT
MORE LIKE JOB

Most of us wouldn't want to go through the spiritual warfare that Job had to endure in his lifetime. He was a good guy, doing what God wanted and practicing his faith, only to find himself in a litmus test. How far could he be pushed before he might give up his right actions toward God? We won't delve into the theology of Job here, but maybe there's a lesson for us, too.

Spiritual warfare continues around us, and we're in the midst of its slings and arrows whether we see them zooming past our heads or not. We cave in more than we realize as the media arrows bombard our homes via TV sets and computer screens and magazines. We may not see the traps being set and the places we might fall, but God does.

We need the patience of Job to endure the knowledge overload we have to endure. Job didn't understand what was going on, but he remained faithful. We're filled with so much CNN and HBO and everything else that we might know too much of what is going on, and we still must remain faithful. Be patient with yourself as you sort out what is true and what isn't. Be patient with God and let Him show you the way.

CONTINUING EDUCATION

There was a man named Job who lived in the land of Uz. He was blameless, a man of complete integrity.

JOB 1:1

The Building Blocks of Patience

Most of us aren't trained to be patient in the things that come our way. It may be helpful then to devise a system of things to think about when our feathers are being ruffled, our minds somewhat vexed, or we simply don't have time to wait in line for the lady using her coupons at the grocery store.

Let's start with:

P for peace, prayer, and positive spirit.
A for attitude adjustment.
T for thankfulness.
I for insight into someone else's day.
E for easing into the moment.
N for not giving in to negative thoughts.
C for caring about ourselves and others.
E for experiencing more grace.

When you're vexed, start with P and go through each thought until you are experiencing more grace. We'll call these the building blocks of patience.

Continuing Education

You will show me the way of life, granting me the joy of your presence and the pleasures of living with you forever.

PSALM 16:11

PEACE

What's Bothering You?

Borrowing from the bookmark of Teresa of Avila, let's look at her wisdom and insight about attaining peace.

> *Let nothing disturb you,*
> *Nothing frighten you.*
> *All things pass,*
> *And God never changes.*
> *When you endure things with patience,*
> *You attain all things that God can give you.*
> *When you have God,*
> *You lack for nothing.*

Perhaps she didn't intend quite on the interpretation given here, but the point is that we can have peace in any situation if we understand that our God, who is the same yesterday, today, and forever, is in control. With God, nothing is impossible, and when we surrender to His will, peace rules our hearts and minds.

Is it time to create a bookmark with this reminder?

CONTINUING EDUCATION

"May the LORD be good to you and give you peace."
NUMBERS 6:26 CEV

COMMIT TO PEACE

Y ou've grown up in a tumultuous world that gives lip service to peace and undermines it at every turn. Waging peace is not our priority, and each of us has some stake in what happens in the future. What part can we play in committing to peace throughout the land where we live?

Like so many things, peace starts at home. In fact, peace starts with you. Peace is first waged in your heart. How much you fight to maintain it may vary from day to day, but your choices to remain at peace influence the world.

What are the weapons of peace? They are prayer, patience, and powerful beliefs in the wisdom and the will of God in your life. When you surrender yourself and put God at the center of your universe, then peace will rule your heart and flow over into the people you live around.

Build up your weapons of peace. The victory is already yours.

CONTINUING EDUCATION

And let the peace that comes from Christ rule in your hearts.
For as members of one body you are called to live in peace.

COLOSSIANS 3:15

Peace without Understanding

O ne of the biggest robbers of our peace is the question, "Why?" Every time we find ourselves questioning and not coming up with an answer, we're somewhat unsettled and we lose a bit of our peace. It's good to be curious and explore questions of human nature to an extent, but where should you draw the line?

Maybe one place to set up boundaries is that place where you're no longer having fun exploring, you're no longer okay about not knowing the whys and wherefores, and you're starting to make your life miserable. Maybe it's time to go back to the beginning and look for the Source that can bring you a sense of peace again.

Philippians 4:6 says this: "Don't worry about anything; instead, pray about everything. Tell God what you need, and thank him for all he has done." If you do this, you will experience God's peace, which is far more wonderful than the human mind can understand. His peace will guard your hearts and minds as you live in Christ Jesus.

Pray for peace.

Continuing Education

May grace and peace be yours,
sent to you from God our Father and Jesus Christ our Lord.
EPHESIANS 1:2

PRAYER

Start Talking

For some, the idea of the right way to pray is somewhat sketchy. Do you have to get into your prayer posture, get out your knee pads, or wait for inspiration? What do you really have to do to make prayer happen?

Prayer and prayer people take on different dimensions. What you do in prayer is about your relationship with God, and your attitude, and your need, and even your personality. The Bible gives a few tips on making prayer happen, but one of the best is simply to invite God into your thoughts and decisions and start talking. He'll be there, ready to listen.

God is available to you 24/7. He doesn't sleep late or get too busy with other issues going on in the world to hear your prayers. When the prophets of old were praying, you can be sure others somewhere were also praying. You are the child of the King, and He's always willing to hear what you have to say.

Isn't it time for you to do more talking?

CONTINUING EDUCATION

When a believing person prays, great things happen.

JAMES 5:16 NCV

BUT CAN I ASK THAT?

Lots of ideas exist about prayer—some have biblical origins and some come from your family or your denomination—but mostly prayer needs to be about you and God. It needs to be a heart thing, precipitated by your love for God and the awareness of the special relationship you share with Him.

Some people believe you really shouldn't pray for things like the right car if you're car shopping or more money in your bank account. But is there really anything that is important to your life that you can't take to God? If it matters to you, it matters to Him. In fact, the greater your relationship is with Him, the more you can share the intimate details.

If you don't ask God for help, you don't know if He has any answers. Take a few days and experiment. Don't experiment in a "Let me test you on this, God," sort of way, but in a "Let me share this with you, God," sort of way. You may find God has more answers than you have questions.

CONTINUING EDUCATION

"So I tell you to believe that you have received the things you ask for in prayer, and God will give them to you."
MARK 11:24 NCV

PLEASE HOLD,
YOUR PRAYERS WILL BE ANSWERED
IN THE ORDER OF YOUR REQUEST

Imagine what it would be like if you put your prayer request on the heavenly prayer hotline and you were put on hold. "Oh, sorry, God is just swamped today, but He'll be back with you soon. You're currently number 84,322,681. Your prayer requests are important to God, so please hold on!"

Sometimes we treat God as though He had a switchboard operator clearing messages and directing calls. We act as though there's too much red tape, and when our prayers aren't answered, we obviously did not get through the system, and God just doesn't have time for us. Therefore, we may as well give up.

The truth is, the switchboard is always open and your call is number one. You are calling into the throne room, and no matter what else your Father has to do, He'll put those things aside for you, because you're His child.

In fact, He's there right now, and it's a great time to get your call in. Your Divine Operator is standing by.

CONTINUING EDUCATION

Ask, and you will receive. Search, and you will find.
Knock, and the door will be opened for you.
Everyone who asks will receive. Everyone who searches will find.
And the door will be opened for everyone who knocks.

MATTHEW 7:7–8 CEV

BIG PRAYERS
MAKE BIG HEARTS

"Love to pray. Feel often during the day the
need for prayer, and take trouble to pray. Prayer
enlarges the heart until it is capable of containing
God's gift of Himself. Ask and seek and your heart
will grow big enough to receive Him."
MOTHER TERESA

Often we find ourselves telling someone with a specific need that the best thing they can do is pray. That's good advice, but it can seem kind of glib when someone's life is in crisis.

Are you always in the mood to pray about things? The question is, Do you need to be in a certain mood to pray, or do you pray and see if your mood catches up?

Mother Teresa seems to be saying that the prayer itself gives us a big enough heart to receive God, to let God into our lives. If that's true, you need to keep praying until your heart overflows. You'll know for sure God is with you then. You can tell your friends that, too.

CONTINUING EDUCATION

We also pray that you will be strengthened
with his glorious power so that you will have
all the patience and endurance you need.
COLOSSIANS 1:11

You Get What You Pray For!

I f you're praying for rain, it's a good idea to carry an umbrella. In other words, when you pray, it's a good idea to agree with God about the thing you're praying about so that you have an expectation of receiving it. The Bible tells us that if we ask, we'll receive, unless of course, we doubt it will happen.

When Elijah prayed that it would not rain, it didn't rain for three and a half years. When he prayed for rain again, the heavens opened up and the crops were restored. You can believe he didn't doubt for a moment that God would honor his request.

Whatever you're praying for, be sure you really want it. Then be sure you really believe it and let God do the rest. If you're praying according to God's will and purpose for your life, you can expect those prayers to be fulfilled. Ask and you will receive.

Continuing Education

The earnest prayer of a righteous person has great power and wonderful results.

JAMES 5:16

PROVERBS

A Little Help from the Past

Proverbs are wise sayings from those who have come before us, learned a thing or two about life, and are willing to share bits of truth. The biblical Proverbs most often attributed to Solomon are filled with guidance that still translates well into our world today. Other proverbs come from teachers around the world, and some may add to your thinking in a positive way.

Thomas Carlyle said, "These wise sayings seem to have some strange power to discover our rich, hidden talents—those hidden seeds of greatness that God plants inside every one of us."

Here's a hint as to how proverbs can be helpful to you: "If you are already wise, you will become even wiser. And if you are smart, you will learn to understand proverbs and sayings, as well as words of wisdom and all kinds of riddles" (Proverbs 1:5–6 CEV).

Begin today by memorizing the first chapter of Proverbs.

CONTINUING EDUCATION

Proverbs will teach you wisdom and self-control and how to understand sayings with deep meanings.

PROVERBS 1:2 CEV

PROVERBS OF COMMON SENSE

Keep in tune with wisdom and think what it means
to have common sense.
Beg as loud as you can for good common sense.
Search for wisdom as you would search for
silver or hidden treasure.

PROVERBS 2:2–4 CEV

Common sense! Doesn't it seem like a rare commodity sometimes? Even King Solomon said we should "beg. . .for good common sense." We're often surrounded by brilliance or philosophies or lofty ideals, but what about plain old garden variety common sense?

We can be masters at computer technology, know incredible facts about keeping our health or converting our funds, and not be able to fill the dishwasher.

Experiment a little. Think about how often you rely on good old-fashioned common sense and how often you're frustrated by those who don't seem to have it. If you discover you aren't relying on this God-given ingredient in your life often enough, beg for more. A little more common sense all the way around has got to be a good thing.

CONTINUING EDUCATION

All wisdom comes from the LORD,
and so do common sense and understanding.

PROVERBS 2:6 CEV

Advice and Planning

Without good advice everything goes wrong—
it takes careful planning for things to go right.

PROVERBS 15:22 CEV

W e're reluctant sometimes to either give or receive advice. We aren't always sure that we should tell someone else what we think might be best for them, and then later we wish we had shared our thoughts. We don't always want to hear advice that others would give us, especially if it's at all contrary to what we are thinking about doing. But then, what help is advice going to be if we only talk to people who confirm what we want rather than what might be good for us to consider?

We can get so unwilling to share honest thoughts with others that we literally stand back and watch them go into a mode of self-destruction. God does not want us to do that. Perhaps a part of loving our neighbor as ourselves is to be willing to risk a little discomfort and go ahead and offer our concerns and advice. You are God's eyes and ears and voice on earth. Your advice regarding someone else's plans may be just what they need.

Continuing Education

Words of wisdom come from the wise, but fools speak foolishness.
PROVERBS 15:2 CEV

Living Today

Look to this day.... In it lie all the realities and verities
of existence, the bliss of growth, the splendor of action,
the glory of power. For yesterday is but a dream and
tomorrow is only a vision. But today, well lived, makes
every yesterday a dream of happiness and
every tomorrow a vision of hope.

SANSKRIT PROVERB

"Today, well lived" is the prize. Look at what you have planned for your day. Are you going to school? To work? To take care of someone? Or out to enjoy yourself? Whatever your plans, what will make today one that you can look at when the sun goes down and say, "Today was well lived"?

When we assign a purpose to the day, it becomes more meaningful. When your days seem to disappear one after the other without notice, it may be that you have forgotten to assign purpose and meaning to them.

If today is well lived, tomorrow offers more hope and yesterday brings a smile.

CONTINUING EDUCATION

Don't brag about tomorrow!
Each day brings its own surprises.

PROVERBS 27:1 CEV

God's Word and You

Everything God says is true—
and it's a shield for all who come to him for safety.
Don't change what God has said!
He will correct you and show that you are a liar.

PROVERBS 30:5–6 CEV

I f you're going to understand this proverb, you may have to practice your listening skills. You have to listen with intention and discernment. When you do, you may discover that God has things to say to you, and He's speaking to you all the time.

If you think God isn't speaking to you, maybe you just need to get quiet enough, take time to listen, turn down the iPod, and ask Him to come into your space so there's time for just the two of you.

Everything God says is true, and He's waiting right now to speak directly to you. Can you hear Him?

❀❀❀❀❀❀❀❀❀❀❀❀❀❀❀❀❀❀❀❀❀❀❀❀❀❀❀❀❀❀❀❀❀❀❀

Continuing Education

Use wisdom and understanding to establish your home;
let good sense fill the rooms with priceless treasures.

PROVERBS 24:3–4 CEV

SERVICE

ARE YOU WILLING TO SERVE?

S ometimes we treat serving others as though it's a separate part of our lives and we'll get to it when we have time. We put it in the same place as diet and exercise, knowing it's a good thing to do, but maybe we'll start that tomorrow.

What if you take another approach? What if you say your prayers early, let God know you are available to Him today, and that you're ready, willing, and able to serve? What would happen then?

When you give God an open invitation to use you, He'll give you the opportunities. He'll equip you for the job and He'll make sure that you never run out of work to do. He'll also reward you by giving you a deep sense of satisfaction and joy over what you've been able to accomplish through His Spirit.

It's all well and good to talk about serving. It's better to serve. Are you ready?

CONTINUING EDUCATION

So, my dear brothers and sisters, be strong and steady,
always enthusiastic about the Lord's work,
for you know that nothing you do for the Lord is ever useless.

1 CORINTHIANS 15:58

SIGNS OF SERVICE

When you look at slogans for companies that offer a service to others, they often say things like, "We aim to please," or "Our customers are always first."

As Christians, we don't put out a service sign, but if we did, what would it say? "I AIM TO PLEASE—AS LONG AS IT'S AFTER I FINISH MY LATEST BOOK OR WHEN MY FAVORITE TV SHOW IS OVER." Or, "WHAT YOU NEED ALWAYS COMES FIRST WITH ME AS LONG AS IT DOESN'T INTERFERE WITH STUFF I'VE GOT TO GET DONE."

It seems like we're about serving as long as it fits into our regularly scheduled plans. If God comes into our space and wants to "interrupt our regular programming" to do something new, we might not be as ready and willing to move.

Think about how and when you want to serve. If you had to put out a shingle declaring your services for the kingdom of God, what would it say? Whatever you do, serve with a glad heart.

CONTINUING EDUCATION

"The greatest among you must be a servant."
MATTHEW 23:11

You Shall Not Live in Vain

Don't we all want to believe that we were meant to be here? We want to know our purpose for living and give something back to the world. We simply do not want to live in vain, without usefulness or some sense of success.

Emily Dickinson put it this way:

> If I can stop one heart from breaking,
> I shall not live in vain;
> If I can ease one life the aching,
> Or cool one pain.
> Or help one fainting robin
> Unto his nest again,
> I shall not live in vain.

We're here to help each other. Whether that means drying a tear of someone close to you or lifting the spirits of one in need or creating a way for someone else to succeed, then that is what you're here for. We exist to be God's eyes, ears, hands, and feet. We exist to share His heart with the world.

Continuing Education

*Continue to show deep love for each other,
for love covers a multitude of sins.*

1 Peter 4:8

Christ Has No Body but You

Christ has no body now on earth but yours;
yours are the only hands with which He can do
His work, yours are the only feet with which He can go
about the world, yours are the only eyes through which
His compassion can shine forth upon a troubled world.
Christ has no body now on earth but yours.

Teresa of Avila

If you think for one moment that nobody needs you—what you are or what you can do—then think again. As part of the body of Christ, you're in great demand. You're part of a family business, and you've inherited some pretty important work to do.

Family businesses generally succeed because the family pulls together toward the same mission with the same values and the same heart for getting the work accomplished. Every person is important. Every hand is needed.

Keep working for the kingdom. Your family needs you.

Continuing Education

There is one body and one Spirit—just as you were called
to one hope when you were called—one Lord, one faith,
one baptism; one God and Father of all.

Ephesians 4:4–6 niv

WHAT NEEDS TO BE DONE?

Let's say that you and two friends just held a very successful party and now everyone has gone home, but the three of you are left with all the work to do to put the house back in order. No doubt, one person will begin to pick up little things here and there, with no real hurry, just beginning to get the process going. Another person will haul out the vacuum cleaner, start putting the furniture where it belongs, and get the floors picked up enough to vacuum. The third person will take note of all that, decide there's nothing he has to do and begin to watch some TV. The two people working will suddenly realize this and stop and suggest the friend help out. Now the friend says, "What needs to be done?"

This party clean-up scene is going on around you all the time. Some people are out taking care of little things and slowly but surely helping to create some better things in the world. Some are taking on the big jobs of cleaning up people's lives and clearing out the old thinking they had before they knew Jesus. Other people are sitting back and letting everyone else take care of things because they can't figure out what needs to be done.

Whichever person you are, pray for some guidance that God will direct your steps to serve Him according to what He knows needs to be done.

CONTINUING EDUCATION

You should work all the harder because
you are helping another believer by your efforts.

1 TIMOTHY 6:2

SUCCESS COMES IN CANS

Imagine you're at the grocery store and shopping for your favorite soft drink in a can and suddenly you see what looks like a new drink. It's in a can, it looks inviting, and it's called Success. You look around, not sure you want anyone else to see this rare thing. You decide to buy every can.

If it were that easy to find success or create success, then you'd never be able to stock enough of it on the shelves. Actually, the sweet taste of success usually has some bitter roots, and those can leave you wondering if it's really worth the effort after all.

The fact is, success does come in cans. It comes every time you say, "I can do this. I can try harder. I can go the extra mile. I can believe in myself. I can trust God for this." Those are the cans for success.

If you're not finding success, then you may have bought into one too many can'ts. You may be looking at why things aren't happening instead of why they are or why they could. The people who believe they can't do it are usually right. The people who believe they can do it find success.

CONTINUING EDUCATION

A longing fulfilled is sweet to the soul.

PROVERBS 13:19 NIV

If You Dream of Success

I t's good to have a dream of success, to have a vision for where you want to go and what you want to accomplish. Setting goals is always important to helping you understand when success has finally arrived. If you didn't have a goal to get through school, graduation would not be much of a reward.

Let's say you want to write a book and you do all the things it takes to be able to write a book. You get a good computer, you learn how to use the word processing program, you have a great idea, you've developed plot lines, and you have all the pieces together. Are you a success? No, because you still have to write the book.

Dreaming about success is not the same as working toward success. The best place to start is in an agreement between you and God about what your work is and what you hope to accomplish. With His leading in your life, you begin to move into it and work with it until it takes the shape of His blessing. Work is what makes dreams succeed. It's how books get into print.

Continuing Education

Commit to the LORD whatever you do,
and your plans will succeed.

PROVERBS 16:3 NIV

ACCORDING TO EMERSON

*Success: To laugh often and much, to win the respect
of intelligent people and the affection of children, to
earn the appreciation of honest critics and endure the
betrayal of false friends, to appreciate beauty, to find the
best in others, to leave the world a bit better, whether by
a healthy child, a garden patch, or a redeemed social
condition; to know even one life has breathed easier
because you have lived. This is to have succeeded.*
RALPH WALDO EMERSON

As you look to God for direction for your life and try to anticipate those things that you can look back on to define your own success, consider some of Emerson's thoughts. Certainly attaining joy and having the respect of those around you is a good thing. Appreciating beauty and finding the best in others puts you ahead of the crowd. Leaving the world a better place in some form or another will help you to be remembered.

What you imagine to be success and what in truth is success for you will be part of your journey with God. The road is ahead of you and starts today.

❊❊❊❊❊❊❊❊❊❊❊❊❊❊❊❊❊❊❊❊❊❊❊❊❊❊❊❊❊❊❊❊

CONTINUING EDUCATION

As long as he sought the LORD, God gave him success.
2 CHRONICLES 26:5 NIV

THE SUCCESS OF YOUR LIFE

Christopher Morley said, "There is only one success—to be able to spend life in your own way."

This approach to success takes its eyes off the world and puts them squarely on you. It says that only you will know when you have succeeded. It won't be that you built a better mousetrap, received another college degree, or married the person of your dreams unless those are the things that define living life in your own way.

What is required is to know in your own heart the moment of your own success. Perhaps this will be the thing about which you stand before God and say, "This is what I did with the talents You gave me. This is how I used my gifts. With Your help, I succeeded. Thank You, Lord."

You've been given many gifts. Some are learned abilities; others are insights gained from experience or knowing the right situations that would allow you to succeed. What will define your success?

CONTINUING EDUCATION

Whatever you do, do well. For when you go to the grave, there will be no work or planning or knowledge or wisdom.

ECCLESIASTES 9:10

TRIALS

WAITING FOR THE RAINBOW

You've weathered a lot of things already and so you understand what cloudy days are like. You know the ones where nothing seems to go right and everyone has an opinion that is different from yours and apparently their opinions are "the right ones."

When funky days come along, it's not easy to pull yourself out of the doldrums they create. You start to wonder if all your efforts are really worth it or if it might be better to just sail away to some other port and not worry about the storms around you.

The fact is that you may be feeling washed out, but you're not washed up. You're still God's child, and He has a rainbow out there for you even yet. The problem we face is that it takes patience and trust to wait for those rainbows. You know it takes both rain and sun before they can appear, so keep looking because there's one just around the bend.

CONTINUING EDUCATION

"I am giving you a sign as evidence of my eternal covenant with you and all living creatures. I have placed my rainbow in the clouds."
GENESIS 9:12–13

The Peaks and Valleys

G. K. Chesterton said, "One sees great things from the valley; only small things from the peak."

Funny how we usually turn that thought around. Somehow we don't think we see anything from the valley, at least when we're standing in it. When you think about it, though, the valley experiences are the ones that cause you to look up, to search for God, and to seek greater things for yourself. The view from the peak, though stunning, may not inspire your thoughts in the same way.

Your life is always going to be about peaks and valleys. Part of the reason for that is that it doesn't require much faith to live in sameness. If you lived in some imagined city where everything is beautiful all the time, you might not recognize the path you need to walk. Conflict may rub us the wrong way, but it's also our best opportunity to shine. You are designed for a purpose, and part of that purpose is to grow in faith and obedience toward God. Embrace peaks and valleys.

Continuing Education

We live by believing and not by seeing.

2 Corinthians 5:7

Don't Give Me Pat Answers

Do you ever feel the slightest bit of rage when you're going through a crisis of some kind, or even just having basic ups and downs and your friends try to encourage you with some nice—but horribly cliché—pat answers? You know they are looking out for your best interest and trying to think of just the right thing to say, and so they come out with a phrase from a Hallmark greeting card and you're not really helped a bit.

Okay, you're helped because you have friends, but sometimes you just don't want to hear another pat answer. One of the least favorite ones is: "Well, it must be God's will for you." The fact that the person you've been dating called it quits or that your car got run into on the street by a drunk driver without insurance is probably not about God's will.

So what's to be done? Pray for understanding, let time help heal things, and have faith that tomorrow will be a better day. Maybe the "sun will come out tomorrow." Whatever the trial, the best plan is to face it, take it to God, and work through it with the One who cares more for you than anybody on this planet ever could. Just keep looking for the real answers.

❈❈❈❈❈❈❈❈❈❈❈❈❈❈❈❈❈❈❈❈❈❈❈❈❈❈❈❈❈❈❈❈

Continuing Education

"Be strong and courageous!"

2 Chronicles 32:7

TRUST

WHERE DO YOU PUT YOUR TRUST?

Figuring out who and what to trust is a pretty important thing as you go out into the world. It's not always easy to recognize the good guys from the bad guys. They all can wear the same disguises.

If you put your trust in yourself, that's a good place to start but not a good place to end. You're sure to let yourself down at one time or another, and then your source for trust will be lost.

If you put your trust in your friends, that's even shakier. They may not let you down, but life moves on and they'll move with it, and you won't always know where to find them when you need them.

If you put your trust in money, you'll always have to be aware of those who might work hard to take it from you, or you'll live at the whims of the economy. That kind of trust can be easily broken.

If you decide to truly trust in God, you won't have to look out to figure out the good guys or look in to figure out yourself; you can just look up because it's the one place you can store all of your heart's treasures.

CONTINUING EDUCATION

I trust in God's unfailing love forever and ever.

PSALM 52:8

IN GOD WE TRUST

S ome years ago, a book came out called *Like a Mighty Wind*. I remember the author commented that as he flew to the United States for the first time from his own country, he was very excited. He was sure that a place that printed "In God We Trust" on their own form of currency must indeed be a Christian country. He was somewhat shocked when he arrived and realized that wasn't necessarily the case.

We somewhat glibly proclaim that we trust in God, though. And sometimes we really mean it, and other times we're not so sure. As you travel within this country or to others, you might pay attention to how much lip service and how much real service seems to be paid to the amount of trust that there truly is in God.

The reason to note that trust is so that you can make a decision once and for all. Will you be one of the ones who can truly say, "In God I Trust"? Let it be more than your motto or a sign on your wall; let it be your truth.

CONTINUING EDUCATION

[Jesus said,] "Don't be troubled.
You trust God, now trust in me."

JOHN 14:1

CAN YOU BE TRUSTED?

Think about the people in your life whom you feel you can trust completely. There probably aren't many, but a few should come to mind.

What about you? Are you someone others can trust? Are you someone God can trust to do His work and listen for His voice? When you gain someone else's trust, it's a gift. It says that they believe in you and value your thoughts and ideas and know that you will look out for their best interests no matter what situation arises. Trust is a significant thing.

Do you remember the first time you felt trusted? Maybe your mom trusted you to go to the market all by yourself to pick up the things she needed, and so you rode your bike there, took her list, and tried to be wise in your choices. Someone trusted you and you didn't want to blow it.

As you continue to build relationships in the world, don't just look for those people you can trust, but be a person others can trust, and even more than that, be a person God can trust. It'll make a difference in everything you do.

CONTINUING EDUCATION

May the God of hope fill you with all joy and peace as you trust in him.

ROMANS 15:13 NIV

WISDOM

WISE OR OTHERWISE

We don't really talk a lot about people of great wisdom these days. In times past, the great sages and learned people of any population helped to shape the thinking of those around them. Today, people are continually talking, but very few are actually wise. Like everyone else, you need to determine what you'd like to be—wise or otherwise.

Proverbs 3:16–18 (CEV) talks about wisdom in the metaphor of an enlightened woman. It says this: "In her right hand Wisdom holds a long life, and in her left hand are wealth and honor. Wisdom makes life pleasant and leads us safely along. Wisdom is a life-giving tree, the source of happiness for all who hold on to her."

Wisdom certainly sounds like something you would want to pursue. Beyond learning, beyond information gathering, grow in wisdom, for it will serve you well all the days of your life.

CONTINUING EDUCATION

Teach us to use wisely all the time we have.

PSALM 90:12 CEV

SPEAKING OF WISDOM

A wise old owl sat on an oak,
The more he saw, the less he spoke;
The less he spoke, the more he heard:
Why aren't we like that wise old bird?
EDWARD HERSEY RICHARDS

Y ou've probably heard the old adage that we have two ears and one mouth so that we'll listen twice as much as we speak. Doesn't really seem to be the way it works, though. We're much quicker to speak first and listen later. Sometimes even as someone is talking to us, we're not really listening because we're planning what we'll say back, so it's like we're already talking. Have you noticed that?

Try spending some focused time today really listening to what is going on around you. Listen to people everywhere you go; listen to the sounds that float through the air and see if you learn anything new. If anyone asks why you're not talking so much, just smile and keep listening.

CONTINUING EDUCATION

If you love Wisdom and don't reject her,
she will watch over you.
PROVERBS 4:6 CEV

CUTTING YOUR WISDOM TEETH

You might not find this entry so exciting since you're just in the place in life where wisdom teeth are sometimes extracted. It's funny that we have this terminology for our teeth that smacks of wisdom somehow.

To run this analogy a bit further, consider another possibility that you might also be experiencing now, in terms of "biting off more than you can chew." Sometimes having more on your plate than you can wisely handle is a necessary thing. Where it breaks down is if you find yourself ten years from now still taking on more than you can safely or wisely handle.

Only you can gauge the wisdom of how many activities you try to handle at once, but keep in mind that too long on overload will put out your fire. Burning out is never a good plan. Be wise because it's not easy to swallow all the things the world will send your way.

CONTINUING EDUCATION

For the wisdom of this world is foolishness to God.

1 CORINTHIANS 3:19

WORK

You May Not Have a Job, but You Have Work

There's an old joke that says something like, "A lot of people stop looking for work once they find a job." The sad part is that there's more truth than poetry to that line.

The truth for you is that whether or not you have a job right now, you always have work to do. Your work is sharing your heart and mind and soul and the things you know about God whenever you have a chance. That means you can do that when you're working at the pizza place or when you're out walking the dog or wherever you are. It's an open job that can come up anytime and anywhere.

Your services are always welcome, always hoped for, but not required. That's the tricky part because this is a volunteer army. You're only asked to be part of it if you're willing and it's part of your heart's desire.

Whatever your job is, your work is always exciting.

CONTINUING EDUCATION

*Do your work willingly,
as though you were serving the Lord himself.*

COLOSSIANS 3:23 CEV

Working and Praying

S ome people spend forty years in a job they don't like. Then they retire and are faced with a spouse they never really got to know. Then they can't figure out what to do with their time and so they become withdrawn.

You don't have to be like some people, though. You can discover your passions and your talents and your dreams and work with those to the glory of God. If you do work for forty years that makes you happy and allows you to shine, you'll never really work a day in your life. You'll simply be living and learning and growing.

When you retire, the person you married all those years before will be the best friend you have in the universe, and you'll find all kinds of things that are still yours to do that God will call you to. You'll rest in His Spirit, laughing and loving your way back to Him. That's the choice only you can make, and it's one that comes from working and praying.

Pray with all your might for the right work, the right mate, and the right way to give glory to God in all that you do. When you look back in forty years, it will be the best prayer and the best decision you ever made.

Continuing Education

Fear God and obey his commands,
for this is the duty of every person.

Ecclesiastes 12:13

WORRY

WHAT'S UP WITH WORRY?

We each have a kind of worry personality. Some people worry about every little thing that goes on in their lives, and you wonder how they get from one day to the next. Other people don't ever seem to worry about anything, and you wonder how they got so lucky.

Though it may be natural to worry about things, the Bible says that we really don't need to worry about anything. In fact, Jesus said in Matthew 6:25, "So I tell you, don't worry about everyday life—whether you have enough food, drink, and clothes."

If we have that instruction, why is it that we worry so much about the everyday things of our lives? The answer is connected to our faith, to our belief in God's willingness to take care of us, in knowing that we really can trust the everyday details to His care. The only way that worry can decrease is if faith increases. You have to hand those worries over to God and trust His desire to fulfill your needs.

What's up with worry? The only thing up is the One you trust with all your heart, mind, and soul. Give those worries to Him.

CONTINUING EDUCATION

Give all your worries and cares to God,
for he cares about what happens to you.

1 PETER 5:7

IMAGINARY TROUBLES

No matter how hard you rack your brain, you probably won't be able to remember what it is that you were worrying about at this time last year. That thing that kept you up at night, filled your waking moments with dread, and wouldn't ever leave your mind probably passed with little or no ceremony whatsoever.

Mark Twain said, "I am an old man and have known a great many troubles, but most of them have never happened."

And so it is. Most of us worry about far more than will ever happen in our lives. You must choose how much and how long you will allow worry to rule your path. You must decide how many days of worry you'll carry at once. God gives you grace for today. He has already let go of yesterday, and He already has plans for you for tomorrow.

When you're having a sleepless night because you've stuffed too many things into your head and you can't shut them off, take a deep breath, pray, and put all your fears in God's hand. Let Him carry them. He'll be up all night anyhow.

CONTINUING EDUCATION

Don't worry about tomorrow. It will take care of itself.
You have enough to worry about today.
MATTHEW 6:34 CEV

LOSING WEIGHT

How much do you weigh today? Have you been exercising? Staying healthy? Doing things that are good for you? Now let's step aside from the physical things and answer those questions by looking at your emotional and spiritual life.

How much does your spirit weigh today? Have you been exercising all your worries and fears and every negative thought possible? Have you been getting a healthy dose of anxiety?

You don't have to carry the weight of the world on your shoulders. That means that you don't have to carry the weight of your family's troubles, your friend's craziness, or your employer's insanity. You don't have to carry any of those burdens and let them weigh you down. So why are you?

If you lay those burdens at the cross and let Jesus carry them for you, you'll feel a lot lighter and you'll lose weight instantly. You can even eat dessert on this diet because the only thing you have to gain is peace of mind.

CONTINUING EDUCATION
"Come to me, all you who are weary and burdened, and I will give you rest."
MATTHEW 11:28 NIV

SCRIPTURE INDEX

OLD TESTAMENT

Genesis
3:8–9 83
9:12–13 172
12:2 27

Numbers
6:24–26 27
6:26 150

Deuteronomy
Joshua 1:9 . . . . .52, 88
24:15 13

2 Samuel
22:37 56

1 Kings
9:4–5 104

1 Chronicles
22:13 46
28:9 100

2 Chronicles
26:5 170
32:7 174

Job
1:1 148
33:4 124
38:12–14 143

Psalms
4:6 129
8:3–4 31
16:11 149
19:1 144

46:10	14
52:8	175
55:22	9
68:4–6	58
90:12	122, 178
95:7–8	29
103:2–3	63
103:13–14	62
116:1–2	48
118:24	47
139:14–16	78
145:13–14	89
147:5	82

Proverbs

1:2	158
1:5	116
1:5–6	158
2:2–4	159
2:6	159
3:16–18	178
3:27–28	115
4:6	179
4:23	96
4:26	36
13:6	32
13:19	168
15:2	160
15:22	160
15:30	109
16:2	38
16:3	169
16:9	24, 76
17:9	64
17:17	68
17:28	34
18:24	69
20:7	105, 108
24:3–4	162
27:1	161
30:5–6	162

Ecclesiastes

    2:24–25 125

    3:1 66

    3:1–3 12

    3:15 125

    6:9 126

    9:10 171

    11:3–4 7

    12:13 182

Isaiah

    1:18 51

    40:29–31 95

    40:31 53

    64:4–5 17

    64:8 . . . . .17, 94

Jeremiah

    10:12 84

    29:11 44

Lamentations

    3:25–27 145

Micah

    6:8 21

NEW TESTAMENT

Matthew

    5:14, 16 130

    6:22 127

    6:25 183

    6:34 . . . . .81, 184

    7:7–8 155

    11:28 185

    12:35 97

14:19 91
13:16–17 42
16:8–9 55
17:20 6
18:21–22 65
19:19 114
19:26 16
23:11 164
25:21 45
29:26 16

Mark

8:36 106
9:23 74
11:24 154
12:30 98
12:31 134

Luke

6:31 71
6:35 22
6:45 33

John

1:3–4 132
1:5 130
1:9 128
1:11–12 79
3:16 118
8:31–32 18
12:25 125
14:1 176
15:14 67
15:22 40

Acts

20:35 72

Romans

5:3–5 . . . . .11, 102
7:21 121

8:28 . . . . .49, 103
12:10 135
15:13 177

1 Corinthians
3:19 180
9:27 117
12:4–6 119
13:1 142
13:11 93
14:1 141
15:58 . . . . .43, 163

2 Corinthians
5:7 173
5:17 37
9:7 70
9:8 90
9:10 73
13:5 50

Galatians
6:2 59
6:9–10 110
6:10 60

Ephesians
1:2 152
4:4–6 166
4:32 . . . . .23, 113

Philippians
4:4–5 85
4:6 152
4:6–7 25
4:8–9 20
4:13 . . . . .10, 35

Colossians
1:11 156
1:16 77

3:12–13................................140, 147
3:14....................................137
3:15................................138, 151
3:16 57
3:23................................39, 181
3:23–24.................................15
4:6 87

1 Thessalonians
3:12...................................136
5:5....................................131

1 Timothy
1:5....................................133
4:12 28
5:8 61
6:2....................................167

2 Timothy
4:22 86

Hebrews
10:36..................................145
11:1...................................101
12:1...............................41, 75

James
1:17...............................120, 146
4:10 8
5:16...............................153, 157

1 Peter
3:8....................................112
4:8................................139, 165
5:6–7 30
5:7....................................183

2 Peter
3:18................................26, 92

1 John
    2:17 80
    3:18–19. 111

3 John
    4. 19

Jude
    2 107

Revelation
    3:18–19 54
    3:20 99